RAILWAY DETECTIVES

*The 150-year Saga of
the Railway Inspectorate*

RAILWAY DETECTIVES

*The 150-year Saga of
the Railway Inspectorate*

Stanley Hall MCIT

LONDON

IAN ALLAN LTD

Photographic Acknowledgements
The photographs used herein are reproduced by
kind permission of W. V. J. Anderson, British
Rail, M. Dunnett, P. D.Hawkins, Hulton-
Deutsch Collection, B. H. Kimber, M. Mensing,
B. Morrison, National Railway Museum, R. M.
Newland, E. M. Patterson, Real Photos, -
S. Rickard, R. Russell, L. Sandler, G. S. Smith,
D. Sutton, M. E. Ware, H. Weston, P. B.
Whitehouse.

First published 1990

ISBN 0 7110 1929 0

Published by Ian Allan Ltd, Shepperton, Surrey;
and printed by Ian Allan Printing Ltd at their
works at Coombelands in Runnymede, England

Contents

Foreword

Railway safety is always a topic of interest, and although today's high standards are mostly taken for granted, any accident may well become headline news, and be read about in the newspapers, or watched on television, along with the other major events of the world that day.

That this is the case has not come about by chance. It has been achieved by the painstaking tasks of detailed investigations, reviews of evidence, recommendations and subsequent changes to rules and equipment to incorporate the advances of modern technology. Like the British legal system, progress has been brought about by basing change on experience, always seeking perfection, and trying to reduce or eliminate human error.

Who are these men who have sought tirelessly to improve our railway system and ensure the highest standards of safety? It can be said that they fall into two groups, but both with the common aim of safety.

Stanley Hall falls into the first of these groups, a railwayman first and foremost, who has progressed far up the operating tree since joining the LMS at Keighley in 1943, through the grade of station master in a number of Regions of British Railways, and thence to Divisional Operating Superintendent at Birmingham, leaving that position to take up the role of Signalling and Safety Officer at the British Railways Board, where he was at the centre of his lifetime interest in railway safety and its application to both regulations and equipment. He had been able throughout the latter part of his career to take an active part in the investigation of accidents and their aftermath, and armed with this experience, to play an important part in shaping changes in safety practices — a job I know from my experience he found most satisfying. Therefore, he belongs to that group of railway people who have studied the rules of the railway with the safety of passengers very much in mind.

This task meant that Stanley Hall had to work alongside the second group of people in this field of railway safety. These are the Inspecting Officers of Railways of the Department of Transport, a group of people with a very long history of dedication in this field; therefore who is better qualified to write about their history and their work than someone who has spent a lot of his career in company with them?

My own father was head of the Great Western Rules Section of the Superintendent of the Line's Office at Paddington, and he also had many dealings with the Railway Inspectorate, so that a lot of the names mentioned in this volume were familiar to me in my schooldays. In later years, when I too joined the railways and eventually became Divisional Manager at Liverpool Street, then Chief Operations Manager of the Southern Region and Deputy General Manager, before going to the British Railways Board as Director of Operations (one month after Stanley Hall retired), and subsequently Director, Safety, I have enjoyed the company of, and working closely with, the people who form the last 20 years of the 150 covered in this book.

During almost the whole of the period, as this volume explains, the Royal Engineers formed the backbone of the Railway Inspectorate, which meant that they had undergone an intensive period of training within the railway industry. It was often at this time that links were forged with the railways and with individuals well before they reached the exalted rank of an Inspecting Officer of Railways. There is no better test of mettle than working alongside a person in a time of high crisis, with perhaps tragedy around, with the common aim of seeking both the cause of an accident, and its remedy.

From my own experience I can testify to the dedication to the task of these officers, and whilst most publicity is attached to the accident inquiries which they hold, and to the reports which they subsequently produce for the Secretary of State, there is another role which is just as important. This other role is the inspection and approval of new railway works, often coupled with an advisory role in their development, and I am pleased to read that this history outlines the part played by individual officers. Many advances in safety have been brought about after pressure from the Inspectorate.

Legislation in recent times has started to bring about subtle changes in the relationship between the Railway Inspectorate and the Railways. Emphasis is turning towards who was to blame, and whether they should be called to account, rather than the identification of the cause and the recommendation of measures to prevent a recurrence. One must be wary that such a change does not introduce a deterrent against the faithful account of events from witnesses at an inquiry, from fear of repercussions. If this were to happen, the true cause may be much more difficult to find in spite of the advances in modern technology which can retrace the immediate events before an accident. Such a development could only hinder the search for improved safety.

The major tragedies of King's Cross in 1987 and Clapham Junction in 1988 also introduced a rarely-used accident investigation procedure under Section 7 of the Regulation of Railways Act 1871. The Secretary of State required that those two inquiries should be undertaken by a member of the judiciary, with the assistance of assessors, rather than by having the inquiries dealt with by an Inspecting Officer, as has been the almost unvarying practice for over 100 years. Only twice previously has a Section 7 inquiry been ordered — the Tay Bridge disaster of 1879 and the Hixon level crossing accident of 6 January 1968. Whether this will set a precedent for future major accident inquiries remains to be seen, but it may subsequently be judged as a landmark, and a not particularly desirable one, in the history of the Railway Inspectorate. Having been directly concerned with the Clapham inquiry during the 59 days in court, 56 of which concerned the taking of evidence with the employment of counsel, I can say that it is a very different proposition from the type of inquiry held by the Railway Inspectorate. Both types of inquiry have their strengths and weaknesses, but all inquiries require detective work.

In any case, the skills required by the Railway Inspectorate of today are somewhat different from those of their predecessors. Modern railway practice has advanced along with the technology which placed men on the moon. Microchips, printed circuits, and the use of computers and their associated programmes, are commonplace in the signalling and traction worlds of today. Investigation in these areas requires a knowledge of them and, as in all professions, it is an ongoing necessity to embrace change and acquire new cultures.

It is fascinating to read of the pioneers in the field of railway safety, and to follow the story through to the present state of the art. I hope all who read this book will appreciate the dedication of the Inspecting Officers, and the railwaymen as well, who have developed the safety systems to the very high level that all passengers enjoy today.

Maurice C. Holmes OBE
Director, Safety
British Railways Board

Railway Inspecting Officers 1840-1990

	Year joined Inspectorate	Year became Chief Inspecting Officer	Year left or retired	No of years' service
Lt-Col (later Gen) Sir J. M. Frederic Smith	1840	1840	1841	1
Lt-Col R. Thomson	1840	—	1840	1
Capt S. C. Melhuish	1840	—	1840	1
Maj-Gen (later Gen) Sir Charles W. Pasley	1842	1842	1846	4
Capt J. Coddington	1844	—	1847	3
Capt (later Field Marshal Sir John) Lintorn A. Simmons	1847	1850	1853	6
Lt-Col (later Gen) George Wynne	1847	—	1858	11
Capt (later Lt-Gen Sir Robert) M. Laffan	1847	—	1852	5
Capt Harness	1848	—	1850	2
Capt (later Sir Douglas) Galton	1850	—	1858	8
Capt (later Sir Henry) W. Tyler	1853	1871	1877	24
Col W. Yolland	1854	1877	1885	31
Capt G. Ross	1858	—	1861	3
Col F. H. Rich	1861	1885	1891	30
Maj-Gen C. S. Hutchinson	1867	1892	1895	28
Col Sir Francis Marindin	1877	1895	1900	23
Lt-Col Sir H. Arthur Yorke	1891	1900	1913	22
Lt-Col G. W. Addison	1895	—	1899	4
Lt-Col P. G. von Donop	1899	1913	1916	17
Col Sir John Pringle	1900	1916	1929	29
Lt-Col E. Druitt	1900	—	1918	18
Lt-Col E. Hall	1919	—	1927	8
Lt-Col Sir Alan H. L. Mount	1919	1929	1949	30
Col A. H. C. Trench	1927	—	1949	22
Lt-Col E. P. Anderson	1929	—	1934	5
Lt-Col E. Woodhouse	1930	—	1949	19
Lt-Col G. R. S. Wilson	1935	1949	1958	23
Brig C. A. Langley	1946	1958	1963	17
Col D. McMullen	1948	1963	1968	20
Col R. J. Walker	1949	—	1952	3
Col W. P. Reed	1953	—	1968	15
Col J. R. H. Robertson	1958	1969	1973	15
Lt-Col I. K. A. McNaughton	1962	1973	1982	20
Maj P. M. Olver	1965	—	1989	24

Lt-Col A. G. Townsend-Rose	1968	—	1986	18
Maj C. F. Rose	1968	1982	1988	20
Maj A. G. B. King	1973	—	—	—
Maj C. B. Holden	1977	—	—	—
Mr A. Cooksey	1982	—	—	—
Mr R. J. Seymour	1988	1988	—	—
Mr D. S. Harland	1989	—	—	—

Notes

1 The first two Chief Inspecting Officers were known as Inspectors-General.

2 Capt Simmons was known as Secretary of the Railway Commissioners.

3 It is difficult to be precise about the dates of some of the earlier Inspecting Officers. Details have been extracted from the Corps of Royal Engineers records, and from the records of the Board of Trade.

Introduction

On 10 August 1990 the Railway Inspectorate of the Department of Transport celebrated its 150th anniversary, having been formed in 1840 'to provide for the due Supervision of Railways, for the Safety of the Public'. That is still its basic role. It acts as a watchdog of safety on behalf of the travelling public.

Not long after the introduction of railways into Britain it became evident to the Government that professional advice was required to enable the Government to judge the various railway schemes brought before them for sanction, and it turned to the Board of Trade for such advice. The Board in turn looked to the Corps of Royal Engineers for a supply of suitably qualified scientific men to act as their advisers.

Initially, an Inspector-General was appointed to examine and report on the projects submitted to the Board of Trade, and he also had the duty, as an Inspector of Railways, of carefully examining all new lines after construction, and of investigating and reporting to the Railway Commission on the causes of accidents. These three responsibilities — advice, inspection and investigation — have been continued, largely unchanged in essence, right up to the present day, a remarkable record of continuity and stability.

However, before venturing on to an examination of the Inspectorate, its members, its activities and its history, it is important to distinguish between the responsibilities of the Inspectorate and the railways themselves so far as safety is concerned, therefore let it be said straightaway that the railways are responsible, wholly and completely, for the safety of passengers. It is for the railways to decide how trains should be operated, what equipment and materials should be used, what rules, procedures and methods should be adopted, how fast trains should run and what the staffing levels should be. The responsibility of the Inspectorate, so far as the safety of the operation of trains is concerned, has never been established by statute, but developed from the reports of successive 19th century Royal Commissions. It is not to supervise the running of trains, but to investigate the causes of accidents and make recommendations, under the powers of the 1871 Regulation of Railways Act. These recommendations do not have mandatory or legal force, and the Inspectorate relies upon persuasion and the weight of public opinion to achieve its ends. Sometimes it is pushing at an open door; in other cases the railways may decline to accept a recommendation because in their view it would cost too much or interfere too adversely in the operation of trains. In the ultimate reckoning these are fundamental matters for railway managers — they have to provide a saleable service at a price the customers are prepared to pay, and it would be pointless for the Inspectorate to make extravagant and unrealistic demands.

In these pages the author would not wish to give the impression that all the improvements in railway safety have stemmed from the activities of the Inspectorate. That would be quite unfair to railway managements, and whilst in the 19th century the Inspectorate had to apply great pressure upon certain railway companies, including some of the largest and most powerful, in order to achieve desirable improvements, in the present century it is mainly the lack of finance which has retarded progress, although it must also be admitted that improvements have not always been made as soon as they ought to have been, particularly in the direction of providing more safety assistance to the driver. In this case railway managements have dragged their feet, despite the Inspectorate's recommendations.

Until the last few years, Railway Inspecting Officers were appointed exclusively from officers of the Corps of Royal Engineers. This practice began because when the Inspectorate was formed in 1840 the Royal Engineers were really the only source of appropriately experienced and available engineers with the necessary degree of status and independence. The Institution of Civil Engineers had only just been formed and its members were heavily engaged in railway construction. The Royal Engineers ceased to have a Transportation Branch in 1965 on the formation of the Royal Corps of Transport, and from that time the army's railway activities have diminished. The practice of appointing Royal Engineers' officers as Railway Inspecting Officers has therefore ceased because the supply of suitably experienced officers has largely dried up, whilst at the same time the Health and Safety at Work Act 1974 has had the effect of considerably enlarging the number of Railway Employment Inspectors in the Inspectorate, thus providing a pool of experience from which Inspecting Officers can be drawn.

The number of Inspecting Officers has normally been four or five, the present ones being:

Mr R. J. Seymour	Chief Inspecting Officer
Mr A. Cooksey	Deputy Chief Inspecting Officer
Maj A. G. B. King	Inspecting Officer
Maj C. B. Holden	Inspecting Officer
Mr D. S. Harland	Inspecting Officer

There are also a number of Assistant Inspecting Officers and Railway Employment Inspectors, and they are supported by a small administrative body of secretaries and clerks. The Inspectorate as a whole reports to the Secretary of State for Transport.

The Inspectorate has the following main functions:

1   The inspection and approval, from a safety point of view, of new physical works, including signalling, on railways carrying passengers.
2   Accident investigation, including the holding of inquiries.
3   Technical advice to Ministers on general railway safety matters.
4   Enforcement of the provisions of the Health and Safety at Work Act 1974 on the operation of railways, under an agency agreement with the Health and Safety Commission.

Within the pages that follow we shall mainly be concerned with item 2 — accident investigation and recommendations. That is not to say that the three other items are necessarily any less important or time-consuming, but is merely a reflection of the fact that a book of this size cannot do justice to all four. It also means that the activities of the Railway Employment Inspectors, who are responsible within the Inspectorate for matters concerning the safety of staff employed by the railways, can similarly only be touched on. Furthermore, and again in the interests of space, the book confines itself to the activities of British Rail and its predecessors. It has not been possible to include London Transport, nor any of the other metropolitan railways, tramways, cliff railways, preserved railways, narrow-gauge railways, etc, which fall within the purview of the Inspectorate, but mention might be made of the Inspectorate's recent involvement in the Far East. The Hong Kong Government approached the British Government to see if the Inspectorate would inspect new railways and investigate accidents in Hong Kong in the same way as it does in Britain. An agreement was therefore drawn up to cover the Hong Kong Mass Transit Railway and the Hong Kong Light Railway in the New Territories, being subsequently amended to include the modernisation of the Kowloon-Canton Railway within the Colony. Mr Cooksey has already held an accident inquiry there, and has had the distinction of having the report printed in both English and Chinese. Similar arrangements also apply to the Singapore Mass Transit Railway.

Practically all accidents on BR are reported to the Inspectorate. This enables a comprehensive watch to be kept on the general state of safety, and on the development of trends, good or bad. Decisions can also be taken on the desirability of advising the Minister that an inquiry ought to be held, so that the Minister can then appoint one of the Inspecting Officers to carry out that duty, or alternatively can require that a more formal inquiry be held. The powers of an Inspecting Officer regarding the holding of an inquiry are clearly laid down in the Regulation of Railways Act 1871 and will be dealt with in these pages at the appropriate time. One of the provisions of the Act is the publication by the Minister of the Inspecting Officer's report of his inquiry. These reports are particularly valuable and have been set out in the same format for many years, as follows:

1   Summary of the occurrence
2   Description of the site, signalling, permanent way and trains involved

3   The evidence of those involved, and of technical officers
4   Discussion of the questions raised
5   Conclusions
6   Remarks and recommendations

Sometimes a history of that type of accident is included. The railway will have carried out its own private inquiry into the accident within a few days of occurrence, and a copy of its report will already have been sent to the Inspecting Officer before he holds his own inquiry. The purpose of an inquiry is to establish the cause of an accident, and where the cause is not clear (eg because the driver has been killed) the Inspecting Officer will base his conclusion on the evidence. He will also be at pains to point out that the establishment of legal responsibility is not a part of his inquiry. It is simply to find out what went wrong and to suggest how it might be prevented from happening again. It is customary for such inquiries to be held in public, although there is no statutory requirement to do so and the Inspecting Officer will use his discretion as to whether he questions any of the witnesses in private. He may wish to do so if, for example, a witness may be reluctant to speak openly for fear of incriminating himself.

The Chief Inspecting Officer issues an annual report on safety, published by Her Majesty's Stationery Office, setting out the year's results and trends, and giving details of the more important accidents which were not the subject of a public inquiry. These annual reports also contain valuable statistical data.

This book is not an official history of the Railway Inspectorate but the author acknowledges with deep gratitude the assistance and encouragement he has received from members of the Inspectorate, both past and present, and for permission to delve into the records of the Inspectorate, which go back to its beginnings in 1840. He also wishes to acknowledge the invaluable help he has received from the library staff at the National Railway Museum, York, and the Institution of Royal Engineers at Chatham.

The author also wishes to record his appreciation of the encouragement he has received once more from his family and friends.

The story which follows is based on a study of those accidents which were significant in that they led eventually to changes in equipment or methods and an improvement in safety. Inevitably, some of the accidents chosen for inclusion are well known, but could not be omitted owing to their significance. However, the author has been at pains to uncover some lesser-known accidents which he hopes will be of interest to readers. A number of the more recent accidents have been covered in detail in the author's two previous books *Danger Signals* (1987) and *Danger on the Line* (1989), and in the interests of space they are not examined in detail in this book.

What follows, then, is the story of the long and sometimes elusive quest for safety in the running of passenger trains on the main line railways of Britain (and occasionally Ireland, at least up to 1922), set against the background of the country's economic and industrial development of which the railways were, and still are, although to a lesser extent, such an integral part. Turn your mind back, then, to Britain at the beginning of that most exciting era — the Railway Age.

The Beginnings

At the end of the Napoleonic wars in 1815 Britain stood supreme in the world, both politically and industrially. There were three main reasons for this. Firstly, the Industrial Revolution had begun in Britain and the lead which had been given to the country by the great inventors of the 18th century was long retained. Secondly, Britain was supreme as a maritime power and there was no other great power to challenge her. She was in a position to capture the markets of the world. Thirdly, Britain was a united kingdom, which gave her a tremendous advantage over the fragmented countries of Europe. The main element that was missing to enable Britain to take full advantage of her favourable circumstances was a better system of inland transport, and there was plenty of capital available for the development of such a system if one could be devised.

In the 50 years before 1815 there had been a great era of canal building, chiefly to carry coal and iron, and roads had been improved by the establishment of turnpike trusts; but transport was still slow, expensive and unreliable. There was a tremendous pent-up demand for something better.

Railways had existed for many years in primitive form, particularly in colliery areas, and as long ago as 1758 an Act of Parliament had been passed authorising the construction of a railway from Middleton to Leeds. The Surrey Iron Railway obtained its Act in 1801 authorising the construction of a railway from Wandsworth to Croydon, for the conveyance of coals, corn, merchandise and commodities, and worked by horses. The promoters had originally envisaged a railway between London and Portsmouth.

Although the early railways used horse traction, steam engines were already in existence. The inventor of a practical steam engine is generally held to have been James Watt, an instrument maker of Glasgow, who patented his invention in 1769, but its application to railways was slow and confined to a few colliery lines. The development of the steam locomotive, which was to revolutionise not only 19th century Britain but also the rest of the world, was yet to come. However, the stage was now set. The means were available, and the money. All that was needed was the catalyst.

There is some dispute as to whether the railway era commenced in 1825 with the opening of the Stockton & Darlington Railway or in 1830 with the Liverpool & Manchester. In its conception the Stockton & Darlington was little more than a colliery railway, to be worked by horses, but even before it was opened the railway company obtained parliamentary powers to use 'locomotive or movable engines', thanks to the intervention of George Stephenson, who became Engineer to the Railway. The line opened on 27 September 1825, when a procession travelled over the route, led by the company's only steam locomotive, the now famous *Locomotion No 1*. The S&DR did not at first provide passenger accommodation on its trains but allowed private contractors to run coaches on the line, pulled by horses. Difficulties soon arose in regulating the times at which trains and coaches should run, and in 1833 the S&DR bought out the contractors. However, by then a much greater railway had entered the stage.

With the growth of the cotton industry the two important towns of Liverpool and Manchester were developing rapidly and the need for better transport facilities between them was becoming more and more pressing. After much hard work and persistence, and despite fierce opposition from landowners and canal interests, the promoters of the Liverpool & Manchester Railway obtained their Act in 1826. In order to decide upon the form of traction to be employed, a public competition was held at Rainhill in 1829, in which five steam locomotives competed. *Rocket*, made by Robert Stephenson, the son of George, was the winner; an epoch-making event which established the steam locomotive as the best means of haulage, a position it retained for over a century. The success of the Liverpool & Manchester was assured.

The L&MR opened with due pageantry on 15 September 1830 and was so successful that businessmen and promotors all over the country began to develop their own schemes. Plans already in process of development received a great boost, and there was an explosion of interest, as demonstrated by the number of railway bills that were introduced into Parliament in the 1830s (including amendments to existing Acts):

1831	15	1836	47
1832	11	1837	64
1833	12	1838	21
1834	16	1839	28
1835	21		

The number of Acts passed for new railways was as follows:

1831	5	1836	29
1832	4	1837	15
1833	5	1838	2
1834	5	1839	1
1835	8		

Among the more famous companies authorised in this period were:

1831	Sheffield & Manchester
1833	Grand Junction
	London & Birmingham
1834	London & Southampton
1835	Great Western
1836	Eastern Counties
	Manchester & Leeds
	Midland Counties
	North Midland
	South Eastern
1837	London & Brighton
	Manchester & Birmingham
1838	Edinburgh & Glasgow

Even though these were the great days of *laissez faire*, when it was felt that businessmen should be left alone to create wealth and not be fettered by laws and regulations, it was also, somewhat surprisingly, a period when Parliament was very active in promoting social improvements, after the passing of the great Reform Bill in 1832. Lord Althorp introduced his Factory Act in 1833, which provided for paid inspectors to be appointed to see that the law was carried out and provided a precedent for the formation of the Railway Inspectorate. Lord Ashby, who later became the Earl of Shaftesbury, devoted his long life to the improvement of the conditions of his less fortunate countrymen, resulting in Acts to prohibit the employment of children as chimney sweeps, and the employment of children under 13 years of age, and women, in mines. The Municipal Corporations Act of 1835 placed the administration of towns on a proper footing and introduced a single type of town council, elected by male ratepayers. It was not surprising, therefore, that the rapidly-developing railway system soon attracted parliamentary attention, and it was felt that some control over the working of the railways was necessary in the public interest. A Parliamentary Select Committee was therefore appointed in 1839 to consider the question and its recommendations led to the Regulation of Railways Act of 1840. This short Act came into force on 10 August 1840, and commenced: 'Whereas it is expedient for the Safety of the Public to provide for the due supervision of the railways . . .'

It contained the following main provisions:

1. No railway may be opened for the public conveyance of goods or passengers without a month's notice being given (Sec 1)
2. Returns of traffic, charges, and accidents causing personal injury are to be made by railway companies (Sec 3)
3. The Board of Trade may appoint persons to inspect railways (Sec 5)
4. Copies of railway bye laws are to be laid before the Board of Trade (Sec 7)
5. Railway servants found drunk on duty, or guilty of misconduct which might cause injury or obstruction, are liable to a fine or imprisonment (Sec 13)

6. Anyone obstructing trains or endangering safety is liable to imprisonment (Sec 15)

Thus was the Railway Inspectorate born, with powers to inspect any railway. The Inspectors were drawn from the Corps of Royal Engineers, a practice which continued until the 1970s. The first Inspector General of Railways was Lt-Col Sir J. M. Frederic Smith, and two other officers were appointed to assist him – Lt-Col R. Thomson and Capt S. C. Melhuish. Sir Frederic Smith held office only until the following year, when he resigned to take up the position of Director at the School of Military Engineering, Chatham. Maj-Gen Sir Charles Pasley, who had been Commandant at the School since its opening in 1812, then took over as Inspector General of Railways.

Facsimile of Letter from George Stephenson

To the
    Right Honble H. Labouchere,
       President of the Board of Trade.

Sir,
    Since my examination before the select committee on Railways I see the difficulties you have to contend with, from the opposing members to your Bill in bringing forward a measure for the management and better regulation of Railways. I am quite sure that some interference on the part of Government is much wanted. Perhaps I ought to be the last man to admit this (the whole system of Railways, and Locomotive Engines have been brought out by my exertions) but when I see so many young Engineers, and such a variety of notions, I am convinced that some system should be laid down, to prevent wild, and visionary schemes, being tried, at the great danger of injury or loss of life to the public. I consider it right that every talented man should be at liberty to make improvements, but that the supposed improvements should be duly considered by proper judges. Then the question follows, from the opponents to the Bill, who are those judges to be? I beg to lay before you my views on this point.
    Suppose any Engineer has any improved plan for the better working of Railways to propose, he should submit his plan to the Engineer belonging to the Board of Trade, but before that Engineer should give his decision as to the utility of the scheme, he should have full power to call together the chief Engineers of the principal Railways of the Kingdom, and after the subject has been duly discussed, votes should be taken for and against the measure: the discussion should be laid before the Board of Trade, accompanied with the observations of the government Engineer, and if approved of should be then placed into his hands to carry out.
    I should propose for the consideration of the different Engineers that the speed of Locomotives should not exceed forty miles per hour on the most favourable Lines, excepting on special occasions: curved Lines to diminish in velocity according to the radius. I am quite aware that this cannot be carried out to any great nicety, but still it would be a check upon the Drivers.

Collateral Lines require government consideration is a very strong point of view.

Uniformity of signals is another desirable point.

As several persons are now turning their attention to the construction of self acting breaks, it will soon appear that great benefit and safety to travelling will be found by their adoption. In the mean time no train should be allowed to travel which has not two breaksmen and four coaches in each train should be provided with breaks to allow for contingencies. It is my opinion that no contrivance can be found out by which the breaks can be dispensed with.

Six wheeled Engines and carriages are much safer and more comfortable to the travellers than four; any person riding one hundred yards upon an engine or coach constructed upon this plan would discover the difference. The rim of all Railway wheels ought to be made the same width, and the axle trees for all coaches of a strength approved of by the Engineers, both wheels, springs, and axles should bear the government stamp, to being made of the best materials, as every practicable means ought to be made use of in order to have these made of the best iron.

All disputes between Railway Companies should be decided by the Board of Trade.

It appears to me that the above suggestions might be carried out with success, without interfering injuriously with Raily property. I hope that you will not consider that I am intruding by sending you these observations.

I am Sir,
Your Most Obt. Servant,
(Sgd.) *Geo. Stephenson.*

Tapton House,
nr. Chesterfield.
March 31st, 1841

The Inspectorate had no powers other than to inspect railways, and they could do nothing if they found that a new railway had not, for instance, been built to a standard that would allow passengers to be carried safely, other than to use their powers of persuasion. A similar situation arose so far as the discovery of unsafe working practices in the operation of railways was concerned. The Inspecting Officers had no powers to insist on changes, nor had they any powers to inquire into accidents, but they did carry out such inquiries without any authority, and their reports bring out clearly the primitive operating methods of the day. This was a matter of considerable importance; by 1841, there were no fewer than 1,556 miles of railway open and over 20 million passengers were carried that year. After the mini railway-mania of the middle 1830s the promotion of new lines had subsided and in 1840, for the first time for several years, no new railway was authorised, and only one was authorised in 1841. There was a feeling that the railway map was reaching finality and that the Inspecting Officers' duties would be mainly concerned with accidents, and with making recommendations to improve safety.

Lt-Col (later Gen) Sir J. M. Frederic Smith FRS
Chief Inspecting Officer: 1840-41

Resigned CIO 1841 to become Commandant School of Military
Engineering. With Professors Airy and Barlow formed Commission that
considered desirability of uniformity of gauge. MP (Conservative) for
Chatham for some years. Lt-Gen 1859. Gen 1863.

The first railway accident which had the distinction of being investigated by
the Railway Inspectorate occurred on 7 August 1840, three days before the
Inspectorate was formed. Lt-Col Sir Frederic Smith inquired into the accident,
which happened on the Hull and Selby Railway near Howden. A heavy casting
which had been loaded on a wagon marshalled next to the engine fell off and
derailed the following coaches. Four passengers were killed.

Maj-Gen (later Gen) Sir Charles Pasley FRS
Chief Inspecting Officer: 1842-46

Fought at Maida. As extra ADC to Sir John Moore in retreat to Corunna
gave his horse to a lamed soldier and finished the retreat on foot with one
boot. Was at Walcheren — badly wounded in siege of Flushing — invalided
for one year during which he learned German. With help from Wellington
started School of Military Engineering in 1812 as Brevet-Major. Retired as
CIO in 1846. FRS in 1816. Lt-Gen 1851. Gen 1860.

A month later, the Up morning train of the North Midland Railway was
derailed between South Wingfield and Ambergate, killing two passengers. The
very next day a train overtook and collided with the train in front at Old Ford,
near Bow, on the Eastern Counties Railway, killing a passenger. The driver was
sacked and the Inspector, Lt-Col Thomson, recommended that there should be
a school for enginemen; that there should be half-an-hour between trains
starting and that mileposts should be erected at the lineside so that passengers
could assess the speed of the train and complain to the railway company if they
thought that it was excessive. If collisions were to be avoided in the absence of a
signalling system it was essential firstly that trains ran to time and secondly that
there was a sufficient interval of time between trains starting.
A collision on 11 November 1840 in which two more passengers were killed
occurred on the York & North Midland Railway at Taylor's Junction (also
known as South Milford Junction) and added to the public alarm already being
felt at the frequency of railway accidents. The 6.04pm passenger train from
Leeds to York and Hull, via Woodlesford, Castleford and Burton Salmon was
standing in the station at Taylor's Junction when it was run into by a following
luggage train. Sir Frederic Smith recommended that no train should be allowed
to pass or leave a station within 10min of the preceding train, during which time
a red flag or lamp should be displayed. There were no fixed signals at Taylor's
Junction and the Inspector-General called for a statement from all railway
companies showing which stations were provided with revolving signal lamps
placed on posts. It transpired that the passenger train did not have a tail lamp

and that the breaksman (sic – the spelling 'brake' did not come into general usage until late in the 19th century) had ridden upon the top of the fourth vehicle and had shown his red handlamp towards the rear. Once again the importance of trains running to time was stressed.

It is interesting to note that when Capt Melhuish inspected the Birmingham & Gloucester Railway he discovered that Down trains used Birmingham time whilst the Up trains used Cheltenham time and that the clocks of those two towns varied by between 10 and 15min. He recommended that all lines of railway leading to London should adopt London time, under the appellation of 'railway time'.

There were two other interesting features of note in 1840. Smoking was not allowed anywhere in trains or on railway premises, and intoxication and trespass were a widespread problem, causing many deaths. Inebriated passengers often fell out of trains, or crossed the railway without taking care and were knocked down. Trespassers had not yet learnt that a railway train is a very effective killer.

The Inspector-General soon became aware that the powers conferred upon him by the 1840 Act were insufficient to enable him to supervise the operation of railways properly. In 1841 he reported on the measures which he thought were necessary, stating that whilst the Government should not attempt to regulate matters of detail and take the management of the railways out of the hands of the directors and their officers, it was necessary that the Government should have the power of enforcing the observance of all precautions and regulations which were approved by experience and were obviously conducive to the public safety. He also said, in relation to the powers in the 1840 Act, that it was essential to prevent a new railway from opening if it was found to be unsafe or unsatisfactory.

As a result of this report, Mr Gladstone, the newly-appointed vice-president of the Board of Trade, introduced another Bill, which became law on 30 June 1842, and was entitled 'An Act for the better Regulation of Railways and for the Conveyance of Troops'. It amended most of the provisions of the 1840 Act and gave the Railway Inspectorate greater powers, which were to be largely unchanged for the next 30 years or so. In particular, Section 6 gave the Board of Trade power to postpone the opening of a new line if an Inspector reported that the opening 'would be attended with danger to the public using the same' by virtue of the works being incomplete, or the establishment for working the railway being insufficient. Section 8 gave the Board of Trade the power to demand returns of serious accidents whether causing personal injury or not. The Act also made provision for safety at level crossings, requiring the gates to be normally placed across the road, rather than across the railway, except where the Board of Trade authorised otherwise.

The 1842 Regulation of Railways Act did not empower the Inspectors to inquire into railway accidents but nevertheless they continued to do so. Similarly, it contained no provisions for the recommendations of the Inspectors, following inquiries into accidents, to be enforced. The Government rightly felt that such powers would take the management of the railways out of the hands of the directors and place the responsibility for safety of operation fairly and squarely upon the Inspectorate and the Board of Trade. This was felt to be an unwarrantable interference in the running of the railways and a dangerous step for the Government to take, a point of view that has prevailed until the present day, except for some specific provisions in an Act of 1889, and which has stood the test of time. This principle, that the railway companies should bear the full responsibility for the safety of operation of their trains, has been questioned several times over the years but has always prevailed.

It is quite likely that attitudes in 1842 were influenced by a continuing reduction in the number of accidents. Indeed, only one passenger was killed that year while travelling by train and exercising the proper degree of caution, out of over 20 million passenger journeys. The railway companies were learning the importance of punctuality, and fixed signals (ie mechanical signals in fixed locations) were coming into use. Stronger carriages were being built and there was a general adoption of the use of buffer springs to help to absorb an impact in the event of a collision.

Provided that trains could be guaranteed to run punctually, and provided that all the trains that ran were in the timetable, there would have been little need for a signalling system, but it was becoming very obvious that these two conditions were unattainable in practice. Locomotives were not sufficiently reliable and were sometimes overloaded; also, they broke down in mid-section between stations, or lost time in running. The safety system that developed consisted of two essential parts: first, there was the principle that a train should not be allowed to pass a station until the previous train had had sufficient time to get well clear; and second, the principle that if a train broke down in mid-section the guard was to go back along the line at once showing a danger signal, such as a red flag or lamp, to warn the driver of the following train.

Primitive signals began to be erected at stations for the guidance of drivers, and staff were employed to operate them. After a train had passed, the signal was operated to show danger for a period of time, possibly five or 10min, then the danger signal was replaced by one showing 'all clear'. At some stations, and on some lines, a caution signal was displayed for a fixed period of time before the 'all clear' was given. Where there were no fixed signals, a policeman gave the driver the different indications by means of hand signals. These policemen were properly sworn-in constables and were required to investigate accidents. They were arrayed in top hats and swallow-tail coats, and even though they were to be replaced by signalmen before many years had passed the name still lives on today in the form of 'bobby', a term frequently used by drivers when referring to signalmen. Another expression still used by drivers, which dates back to those early days, is the word 'board', used to describe a semaphore signal. Early signals were often wooden boards, which were turned to face the driver to indicate 'danger', and were turned end-on for 'all clear', which was sometimes indicated by a disc. These disc and crossbar signals were very popular for a time but went out of general use over a century ago.

Detonators, which are small explosive devices clipped to the rail-head in an emergency and exploded by the wheels of a locomotive passing over them, were invented in 1841, and rapidly came into use to enable guards of broken-down trains to give an extra warning to drivers of following trains. They were especially useful in fog, when the red light from the guard's handlamp was easily overlooked by a driver peering ahead into the gloom. Fusee signals were also used from an early date. They were similar to roman candle fireworks and were placed on the track to indicate that a train had been stopped there in mid-section and had since moved on but may be somewhere just in front.

The first half of the 1840s was a period of consolidation. In 1841 there were 1,556 miles of railway open for traffic, and 20.4 million passengers were carried that year. By the beginning of 1845 the mileage open had increased to 2,240, and passengers carried to 30 million. These were small increases, compared with what was to follow. Only 10 Acts were passed for new railways in the first half of the 1840s and the Inspectors were only examining about 200 miles of new railway each year, prior to its opening.

So far as safety was concerned, in 1843 only one pasenger was killed in a train accident (a collision at Barnsley on the North Midland Railway in fog; he was the only passenger on the train), whilst six were killed in 1844 in four separate accidents. On 2 September that year it is recorded that no fewer than 5,600 passengers travelled from Sheffield to Hull in four excursion trains. There was a slight collision between two of the trains and a passenger sitting *outside* one of the carriages was thrown off and killed. All the passengers had been put inside the carriages before the trains left Sheffield but some had climbed out on the journey to escape the crush.

There were two accidents in 1844-45 which were forerunners of some which still happen today. A train ran into a cow on the line at Ryton on the Newcastle and Carlisle Railway. The engine was thrown down an embankment and the driver was killed (a cow caused a derailment at Polmont on the Edinburgh to Glasgow line in 1984 and 13 passengers were killed). A passenger was killed in another accident when an engine which was going to assist a train that had broken down ran into it, a type of accident not unknown in the 1980s.

The electric telegraph was coming into widespread use by the mid-1840s as a means of giving information about the running of trains. It was first brought into use on the Blackwall Railway and on the Great Western between Paddington and Slough, but by 1845 it was in use on the whole of the London & South Western Railway and the South Eastern Railway, on most of the London & Birmingham Railway, and was being ordered or installed on other railways. Electric telegraph block signalling was first installed in 1844 on the Norwich-Yarmouth line. But perhaps the most significant comment on the year 1845 was that no fewer than 2,746 miles of new railway were authorised in that year's parliamentary session (although even that figure pales into insignificance compared with the 4,538 miles which were authorised the following year — however, a lot of the mileage authorised was never actually built). The railway mania was about to engulf the country, as illustrated by the enormous expansion of railways which took place in the second half of the 1840s:

Year	*Mileage of railway open for traffic*	*No of passengers (million)*
1846	3,142	
1847	3,945	44

Year	Mileage of railway open for traffic	No of passengers (million)
1848	5,127	58
1849	5,996	64
1850	6,621	67

Despite the massive increase in mileage and traffic, the number of passengers killed in train accidents from causes beyond their own control remained low. Nine were killed in 1848, five in 1849 and 12 in 1850. These figures are all the more remarkable when one considers that the new railways were largely run by staff with little or no experience, and that some of the more impecunious lines could afford neither proper safety appliances nor adequate staff.

Field Marshal Sir J. Lintorn A. Simmons GCB, GCMG

John Simmons was born in 1821, and was gazetted as a Second Lieutenant in the Corps of Royal Engineers in 1837. He passed through the officers' course under Col Sir Charles Pasley and was ordered to Canada in 1839. Returning to England, he was selected in 1847 for the appointment of Inspector of Railways, succeeding to the post of Secretary of the Commission in 1850. In 1851 the Railway Commission was abolished and its duties were handed over to the Board of Trade, when Simmons became the first Secretary of the Railway Department under the Board.

Simmons obtained leave in the autumn of 1853 to travel in Eastern Europe, where relations between Russia and Turkey were becoming strained. When war broke out Simmons immediately became involved, reporting on the condition of the Turkish defences. His leave then having expired he was preparing to embark for England, when the war took a serious turn and he became deeply involved again. He then received, almost in the midst of battle, a communication directing him to return at once to England or resign his appointment as Secretary of the Railway Department. Capt Simmons was in his element in the war with Russia, and only one answer was possible. Without hesitation he sent in his resignation, and resumed what became a brilliant army career of great interest, but unfortunately outside the pages of this book.

In 1848 the Inspectorate consisted of Captains Simmons, Harness, Laffan and Wynne. They were kept extremely busy not only inquiring into accidents and inspecting new lines, but also inquiring into all manner of disputes between railway companies and between railway companies and local authorities. In 1848 they examined and sanctioned the opening of 1,191 miles of railway, in 116 separate inspections.

The worst accident in 1848, in fact one of the worst to date, occurred on the Great Western Railway at Shrivenham on 10 May. The porters were moving wagons in the sidings, and one of the wagons, a horsebox, inadvertently fouled the Up Main line. The policeman had already cleared his signals for a West Country to Paddington express, which was approaching at 55-60mph, consisting of three first-class carriages, three second-class carriages and a luggage van, hauled by an eight-wheeled engine. The express dashed into the horsebox and smashed it to smithereens, then became derailed. The carriages piled up in a heap. There were three important lessons to be learned from this accident:

1   There were no trap points or scotch blocks to prevent vehicles in the sidings from escaping on to the main line.
2   The fixed signal was not interlocked with the sidings points.
3   The braking system in use on the express was inadequate for such a high speed. The only brakes available apart from those on the engine and tender, were hand brakes operated by brakesmen riding in the train. It was to be many years before adequate braking systems came into general use.

A similar accident occurred on the same railway at Wootton Bassett, not many miles away, in 1850. An excursion train returning to Bristol at 10.45pm, and running at 25-30mph, collided with a horsebox which had run out of a siding. The magistrates found the policeman on duty guilty of neglect for not examining the vehicles in the sidings and ensuring that they were secured. He was sent to prison for his offence. Following these two accidents the GWR decided to provide short dead-ends or scotch blocks at all locations.

The new railways were immensely popular with the working classes, who used them in large numbers. Excursion trains were very frequently run, but they were more than ordinarily prone to accident for a number of reasons. Owing to the enormous crowds who sometimes used them the trains were often of great length, overpowering the engines provided. They did not run to a fixed timetable and therefore they were particularly vulnerable. However, partly because of the low speeds at which they ran, some of the accidents had their comic side, though no doubt they were frightening at the time to the passengers. A Whitsuntide excursion in 1849 returning from Liverpool to the East Lancs Railway came to a stand near Burnley because the engine was underpowered. As it had been travelling very slowly, the following regular passenger train caught up and collided with it at low speed. The guard of the regular train ran back to protect his own train, but he did not get far enough to prevent a third train, a return excursion from Preston, from colliding with the regular train. The return excursion from Liverpool consisted of 32 carriages with an engine *at each end*! There were no serious injuries.

Tragedy was also narrowly avoided in another incident the same year at Whiston, on the Liverpool and Manchester section of the already mighty London & North Western Railway. A passenger train collided at low speed with the rear of a train of empty cattle trucks. The guard ran back and managed to stop a following goods train in time. The goods guard ran back and managed to stop a following Manchester to Liverpool express, whose guard then did the same with another express from Preston and the North to Liverpool. There were thus five trains nose to tail. Capt Laffan severely criticised the LNWR for allowing trains to pass the previous station at such short intervals, but the redoubtable General Manager of the LNWR, Capt Mark Huish, did not accept these strictures and a disputatious correspondence followed. The LNWR was already the largest railway in the country, a position it was to claim throughout its life until it formed part of the London Midland & Scottish Railway group in 1923.

In a report on a collision at Woodlesford in 1850, on the Midland Railway a few miles south of Leeds, there is reference to a 'distance' signal. An excursion train of 40 carriages, returning to Leeds about midnight from the Doncaster races, was run into at low speed whilst it was unloading passengers in the station. The station signal was at danger, but the lamp at the distance signal had not been lit and was not seen by the driver of the following train. Distance signals were beginning to be used because there had been so many cases of trains running into other trains standing in stations and not fully protected by the station signal. A distance signal was therefore provided a few hundred yards in rear, and drivers were supposed to stop at it if it showed 'danger'. They were then allowed to proceed past it cautiously, in case there was a train in front. The distance signal was regarded as a 'stop' signal, but drivers frequently passed it without bothering to come to a complete stop, and there were several collisions over the years as a result. Eventually the distance signal became a 'caution' signal, but that was some time in the future.

Statistical Summary 1841-1850

Year	Mileage of railway open for traffic	No of passengers (million)	No of passengers killed in train accidents, through no fault of their own
1841	1,556	20.4	1
1842	1,717	21.4	1
1843	2,036	25.6	6
1844	2,240	30.4	6
1845	2,536	33.8	4
1846	3,142	n/a	3 (last six months)
1847	3,945	44	14 (first six months)
1848	5,127	58	9
1849	5,996	63.8	5
1850	6,621	66.8	12

Finally, in 1850, an excursion train consisting of 18 covered carriages, three open cattle trucks and three open sheep trucks, was run into whilst at a stand near Cowlairs (Glasgow). The guard had omitted to go back to protect his train. The six open trucks had been provided en route to accommodate passengers who refused otherwise to get off the roofs of the covered carriages. Sadly, five passengers in the rear truck were thrown out and killed by the force of the collision.

By now the railway mania had burnt itself out. Only 16 miles of new line were authorised by Parliament in 1849, and only eight miles in 1850. There were over 60,000 railway employees, but in addition 104,000 workmen were employed on building new lines, a figure which itself showed a sharp drop from the quarter of a million thus employed a year or two earlier.

At the end of 1850 there were 6,621 miles of railway open, consisting of 5,132 miles in England and Wales, 951 miles in Scotland, and 538 miles in Ireland. The duties of the Inspectorate, and the provisions of the Regulation of Railways Acts, applied equally to Ireland until the Irish Free State was formed in 1922.

Lock, Block and Brake — the Battle Lines are Drawn

At the beginning of 1851 the Inspectorate consisted of Capt Simmons (Inspector-General), Capts Laffan and Wynne, and Lt Galton. They had done their duty well and had firmly established a pattern of work of the Inspectorate which was to last more or less unchanged for many years. These men were pioneers, especially in the field of accident investigation, which they carried out with great thoroughness and tenacity of purpose despite the lack of any real statutory authority. As they retired, or returned to active service, they were replaced by four more officers of the Corps of Royal Engineers, each one of whom became eventually the Chief Inspecting Officer (previously known as Inspector-General). All four new officers served for more than 20 years and their collective contribution to the improvement in the safety of railway passengers was incalculable. When the first of the four, Lt Tyler, joined the Inspectorate in 1853 railway operating and signalling methods were primitive and accidents were frequent. When the last of the four, Maj-Gen Hutchinson, retired in 1895 the railways had developed into a highly organised, well disciplined and responsible industry, with, generally, a proper regard for safety. The change was not achieved without a struggle, as these pages will show.

Capt Sir Henry Whatley Tyler KCB
Chief Inspecting Officer: 1871-77

Henry Tyler, eldest son of the Deputy Lieutenant of Gloucestershire, joined the Royal Military Academy in 1842 at the age of 15. After training he spent four years in St Lucia as private secretary to the Civil Governor, and was one of several Royal Engineers officers specially employed in the great International Exhibition of 1851. A collection of permanent exhibits he had formed there, afterwards became the nucleus of the South Kensington Museum.

In 1852 he married the daughter of Lt-Gen Sir Charles Pasley and at the same time was appointed engineer to the Colony of Victoria. He never got there, owing to ship breakdowns, and he accepted the appointment of Inspector of Railways in 1853, at the early age of 26.

In 1867 he spent his leave making an inspection of the Grand Trunk Railway of Canada, and spent his following year's leave constructing the first railway in Greece, hiring six brigands to police it. In 1875-76 he was chairman of the English Channel Tunnel Commission, and so far from regarding such a tunnel as a menace to our insular isolation, he held that if only we could induce a hostile army to enter a pipe 30 miles long and 30ft in diameter, it would be worth while spending three million on the construction for that sole purpose.

Capt Tyler's annual reports on railway statistics and accidents became text books of great value, and were studied and quoted in all civilised countries. In 1871 he inspected the International Bridge over the Niagara river, and reported on the Metropolitan water supply. In 1872 he gave evidence on the Euphrates Valley Railway scheme and in 1874 inspected the Erie Railway. The next year he was inspecting railways in Roumelia and Bosnia on his annual leave, a very adventurous busman's holiday!

In 1877 he resigned his appointment as Chief Inspector of Railways, receiving a Knighthood for his services, and became chairman of the Westinghouse Brake Company in England. Tyler was Conservative MP for Harwich for 1880-85 and for Great Yarmouth from 1885-92. He died in 1908.

Throughout his long life Tyler combined great energy and zest with lucidity of thought and clear judgement. He was one of the very few Inspecting Officers to leave before attaining 65 years of age and he was a great loss to the Inspectorate. Had he remained, his influence on railway safety would have been profound. He would have served for a record 39 years and would have been Chief for 21 years. He was followed by another remarkable character — Francis Marindin, of whom more later.

The railways were never dramatically unsafe. Even in the primitive years of the 1850s, the average number of passengers killed in train accidents, from causes beyond their own control, was only about 20 a year, which cannot be considered serious when set against the number of passengers carried each year (85 million in 1851, 150 million in 1859).

The railway companies were reluctant to spend large sums on improving safety. They had to consider the owners, who were the shareholders, and the first duty of the directors was to them. The shareholders had invested in railway companies in the expectation of dividends. If the dividends were unsatisfactory investment would decline or even cease altogether. Companies would wither and die. Decisions about how much to spend on safety were always difficult and never became easier. This was (and still is) an area where the Inspectorate played such a vital role in establishing standards of safety, and in applying pressures to persuade laggard railway companies to comply. The less prosperous lines could barely afford to do so; the more prosperous could, and ought to, have spent more than they did. The four Inspectors who were concerned in these developments were:

Lt H. W. Tyler	1853-1877	24 years
Lt-Col W. Yolland	1854-1885	31 years

Capt F. H. Rich   1861-1891   30 years
Lt-Col C. S. Hutchinson   1867-1895   28 years

Col W. Yolland CB, FRS
Chief Inspecting Officer: 1877-85

Yolland was commissioned in the Royal Engineers, became a Lieutenant-Colonel in 1855 and Colonel in 1858.

His 31 years' service with the Railway Inspectorate, 1854-85 including the final eight as Chief, is a record which seems unlikely to be broken, and he died only shortly before he was due to retire in 1885. A colourful and fiery character, he had immense influence on the development of railway safety during its formative years.

Col F. H. Rich
Chief Inspecting Officer: 1885-91

Rich joined the Royal Engineers in 1840, became a Lieutenant-Colonel in 1867 and a Colonel in 1873.

His 30 years' service with the Railway Inspectorate, 1861-91, was to some extent overshadowed by those two giants Tyler and Yolland, but he finally became Chief in 1885 on the death of Col Yolland.

Maj-Gen Charles Scrope Hutchinson CB
Chief Inspecting Officer: 1892-95

Charles Hutchinson was commissioned as a Second Lieutenant in the Royal Engineers in 1843. For many years he was at the Royal Military Academy, Woolwich, as an instructor in, then later as Professor of, Fortifications, until 1867 when he was appointed an Inspector of Railways. By then he had reached the rank of Lieutenant-Colonel, and retired from the army in 1877 with the honorary rank of Major-General.

During his time with the Railway Inspectorate, from 1867 to 1895, he held 1,100 inquiries into railway accidents, made 6,500 inspections, and travelled on duty 1,250,000 miles. During the building of the Forth Bridge, which lasted seven years, he made an inspection of the work every quarter in conjunction with Maj Marindin, and he was created a Companion of the Order of the Bath by Queen Victoria in 1890 in recognition of that work.

One of his colleagues at the Board of Trade wrote of him:

'He had a passion for work, in the execution of which he displayed a zeal, amounting to enthusiasm. He never spared himself, and often after a comfortless night journey in cross-country trains, he would snatch a hurried breakfast at some dreary railway buffet, and begin a long day's work of inspection at eight o'clock in the morning, much to the surprise and not always to the joy of the railway officers, who wondered how in the world he got there. He gained the warm friendship and respect not only of his colleagues, but also of all the officers of the railways of the United Kingdom with whom he was brought into contact in the course of his official duties.'

For the next 40 years the battle was fought on three main fronts, known as 'lock, block and brake'. 'Lock' might be interpreted for our purposes as the interlocking of signals and points, so that it is impossible for an unsafe combination of the two to be made; and the securing (or locking) of facing points so that they cannot be moved as a train passes over them (facing points are those which can change the direction of a train approaching them). There are four main requirements for safety so far as points are concerned:

1   The points must be fitting correctly, ie the point blade must be lying against the stock rail.
2   The points and the signals must be interlocked so that a signal can only be 'cleared' for the direction in which the points are lying.
3   Once the junction signal has been 'cleared' it must be impossible to move the points.
4   As the train passes over the facing points it must be impossible for them to move even if the signalman has put the junction signal back to danger.

'Block' signifies a space-interval signalling system. In 1851 the use of the time-interval system was routine. Generally it provided that the policeman (or signalman) gave a danger signal for 5min after a train had passed, in order to stop a following train; then a caution signal for 5min more as a warning to the driver of a following train; then an all-clear signal. The fatal flaw in this system is obvious. If a train broke down in mid-section there was a clear risk of a following train running into it. If a train ran slowly the same risk arose. A means was needed of keeping a space between trains so that they could not collide, and this led to the slow development of a signalling system known as the block system, which will be explained later.

'Brake' speaks for itself. It seems quite astonishing now that the primitive braking systems in use in the early days of railways lasted for so long. The only brakes available to the driver, apart from putting his engine into reverse gear, were handbrakes on the tender and on those carriages on the train which were accompanied by guards or 'breaksmen'. The latter rode outside the carriage and screwed on their brakes either in response to the driver's brake-whistle, or when they apprehended danger. Despite the increasing weight and speed of trains during the 1850s and 1860s few real improvements had been made in train-braking systems by 1870 and we shall have to wait until the next chapter for that development.

Primitive operating methods were not the only cause of accidents, as we shall see when we explore some of them during these two decades. Boiler explosions were common and broken tyres and axles were often a cause of serious derailment, sometimes resulting in several deaths and many injuries. However, as engineering technology developed, these causes of accidents declined in frequency.

In 1851 there were 6,890 miles of railway open for traffic, and 85 million passengers were carried. By 1861, the figures had risen to 10,870 miles and 174 million passengers, and by 1871 15,376 miles and 375 million. Freight was more important than passengers in terms of revenue — £26.5 million for freight as against £20.6 million for passengers in 1871. This was a time of great prosperity in industry, and Britain was still the pre-eminent nation, a situation that would not have been possible without the railways. The whole life of the country had come to depend on them, and the use of roads and canals declined. Little wonder, therefore, that railways and the safety of passengers were very much to the forefront of the public and parliamentary mind.

It might be thought that in the 1850s the working man had neither the time, the energy nor the money to take an excursion or travel by train at all, but this was not the case. Horse-racing drew immense crowds, as illustrated by the circumstances of an accident at Sutton Tunnel near Frodsham, on the Birkenhead, Lancashire & Cheshire Junction Railway on 30 April 1851. After the Chester Cup Race no fewer than 9,000 passengers presented themselves at Chester station for the Warrington direction. The station master despatched seven trains, of which the first and second got through without mishap. The third train, however, was too heavy for its locomotive and it ground to a halt near Sutton Tunnel; the fourth was brought up behind to push it along. The combined load proved too much. The cavalcade struggled slowly into the tunnel but speed kept falling and eventually the two trains came to a dead stand, leaving the 2,000 passengers stranded in the eerie smoke-filled darkness. It was pitch black; there were no lights in the carriages but, worse still, there was no tail light. The guard should have gone back to protect his train but failed to do so. The station master at Frodsham, even though he had seen the two trains struggle to get into the tunnel, allowed the fifth excursion to proceed only 5min later. Disaster was inevitable. The fifth train entered the tunnel at speed, to the terror of the stranded passengers as the full realisation of their impending doom burst upon them. In the resulting crash six passengers were killed. But what of the sixth excursion, which was close behind and was again allowed by the Frodsham station master to proceed? Would it too plunge into the tunnel and add to the chaos, with 3,000 passengers milling around in the darkness? Fortunately not. The guard of the fifth train rushed back, frantically waving his handlamp, and managed to stop the sixth train.

Capt Laffan was not sparing in his criticism. He recommended that:

● The block telegraph should be installed between the stations at each end of the tunnel, and no train should be allowed to enter the tunnel until the previous one had passed through it.
● More staff and engines were needed. In a period of rapid expansion suitable and experienced staff were hard to come by, and the resources of both rolling stock and men could be overwhelmed on a small railway company by such a popular event as the Chester Cup Race.
● Lights should be provided in the carriages of trains when passing through Sutton Tunnel.
● The 5min time interval in operation at Frodsham was too small.

Serious accidents in tunnels were not unknown, and there was to be another one at Clayton Tunnel on the London, Brighton & South Coast Railway, 10 years later on 25 August 1861. Again excursion trains were involved, but this time the electric telegraph was already in use through the tunnel. However, there was a different problem — the distant signal for the cabin at the south end of the tunnel had failed in the all-clear position. This type of signal, known as a Whitworth's signal, was designed so that it could be returned to danger either by the signalman turning a wheel acting on a wire, or by the operation of a treddle (sic), placed on the inside of the rail at the signal, which was pressed down by the flanges of the wheels of a train. If the signal failed to operate properly and return to danger an alarm bell sounded in the signal cabin. These safeguards were years ahead of their time but were nullified firstly by the unreliability of the equipment and secondly by the failure of the signalman to respond to the alarm bell in sufficient time.

After the first excursion train had passed the distant signal, it failed to return to danger and the alarm bell sounded. However, the signalman did not respond quickly enough and the second excursion was upon him before he did anything. Coming to his senses in a flash he waved his red flag at the driver just as the engine passed his signal cabin. Seconds later the train plunged into the tunnel. The signalman waited anxiously, but before long he received the 'tunnel clear' message on his telegraph instrument. It was for the first excursion, but owing to a misunderstanding, the man at the south end understood it to refer to the second excursion. He therefore gave 'clear' signals to the driver of the next train, the booked passenger train from Brighton. It entered the tunnel at full speed.

Meanwhile, what of the second excursion? Had it cleared the tunnel? Or had it stopped, directly in the path of the Brighton train? In fact, it had done neither. Its driver had, after all, just caught a glimpse of the signalman's red flag before his train entered the tunnel. Brakes screaming, it eventually stopped safely a good half-mile inside the tunnel, much to the driver's relief. Then, unaccountably, instead of staying where he was and sending the guard back to protect the train and find out what was wrong, he started to propel his train back towards the tunnel mouth. It was not long before he met the Brighton train, which was coming towards him at full speed. There was a fearful crash in the darkness, at a closing speed of at least 30mph. Of the 589 passengers in the two trains, 23 died and 176 were seriously injured, in Britain's worst railway disaster up to that time.

Capt Tyler (now promoted from lieutenant) severely criticised the LB&SCR for allowing trains to follow each other at such short intervals. The reputation of the block telegraph suffered from this accident, but Capt Tyler argued that what was needed was a better block telegraph system, such as was in use on some other railways; a plea that he and his colleagues were to repeat many times in the years to come, and which appears to have been first voiced by Capt Simmons in 1851. The LB&SCR replied to this criticism by suggesting that the widespread introduction of the electric telegraph might make drivers less careful, as it transferred some responsibility from them, and that more danger might be created as a result. This specious argument has been used many times since when measures have been proposed to help the driver.

The worst railway accident prior to Clayton Tunnel had occurred on the Great Southern & Western Railway (Ireland) in 1853, and demonstrated again the need for a space-interval system of signalling, referred to by Capt Simmons in 1851 as ensuring that 'no two trains shall be on the same line at the same time', a principle that was still laid down in the Train Signalling Regulations a century later, and learned by heart by every trainee signalman. An express passenger train from Cork and Killarney to Dublin had stopped about half a mile short of Straffan station, with an engine defect. It was dark but the tail lamp was unlit and there were no side lamps (which ought to have been provided on trains likely to be out after dark, showing a red light to the rear and a white light to the front). The guard went back with his hand lamp to protect, but its dim red light was not noticed by the driver of a following goods train, which crashed into the stationary express at 30mph killing 14 passengers.

A collision at Lewisham on the South Eastern Railway on Sunday 28 June 1857, in which 12 passengers were killed, demonstrated again that the installation of the electric telegraph did not by itself guarantee safety. It had to be accompanied by a proper working system operated by competent staff. This accident also clearly showed yet again the inadequacies of the distant signal as operated at the time.

The 9.15pm Up passenger train from Strood, not due to call at Lewisham, was standing between the distant and the station signals because the station master dared not let it enter the station owing to the great crowd of passengers waiting there. The 9.15pm train, already full, could not proceed through the station until the junction ahead was clear for it. Whilst it was waiting it was run into by the following 9.30pm from Strood. In addition to the 12 passengers who were killed, 62 were more or less seriously injured.

The accident should have been prevented in three ways:

1   The electric block telegraph system in use should have required the 9.30pm train to have been held back at the previous station, but the signalman made an error.

2   The driver of the 9.30pm train should have stopped at the distant signal and then proceeded cautiously past it, ready to stop short of any train that might be in front. However, that rule was habitually broken and the driver of the 9.30pm was no exception. Not only did he not stop at the distant signal but he did not even keep a sufficiently good lookout ahead. He was subsequently arrested and taken to Newgate prison, being later tried for manslaughter at the Central Criminal Court. However, not only was he acquitted, as happened to other drivers in later cases, but both the judge and the jury criticised the management of the South Eastern Railway, a view with which Col Yolland completely agreed. The SER disputed many of Col Yolland's findings and tried to shift the blame on to its staff, but Yolland would have none of it.

3   The guard of the 9.15pm train should have gone back to protect his train but he only went 100 yards. It was not quite enough. Even though the collision

occurred at only 10mph telescoping took place, increasing the number of deaths and injuries.

Concern about the level of safety on the railways was often expressed in Parliament. In 1853 the Cardwell Committee considered whether it was desirable to give the Board of Trade power to enforce the application of an Inspecting Officer's recommendations (an issue which has been raised at intervals ever since) but decided that the balance of advantage lay in leaving the responsibility with the railway companies. The question of the provision of communication between passengers and those in charge of a train was a very live issue during this period, and a House of Commons Select Committee, set up in 1857 to inquire into the causes of railway accidents, recommended the provision of such equipment. However, the railway companies' response was lukewarm, and they had eventually to be compelled to fit such apparatus by the Regulation of Railways Act 1868 on all trains travelling more than 20 miles without stopping. The Act stipulated that the type of apparatus provided had to be approved by the Board of Trade.

As the railways were by now such an integral and indispensable part of everyday business, industrial and social life it is not surprising that railway matters were always well to the fore in the public mind. The desirability of compelling the railways to adopt the Block System of signalling, and the interlocking of points and signals, was often urged but the Devonshire Royal Commission of 1865 pointed out that only 23 passengers had been killed that year in accidents beyond their own control, out of 252 million passengers carried, and that as no other mode of locomotion known to man had shown a more satisfactory result they were not prepared to suggest any alteration in the law. They did however recommend that Inspecting Officers should have the power to require the attendance of officers and servants of railways as witnesses at accident inquiries, and to require the production of books and documents. Both these provisions were incorporated in the 1871 Regulation of Railways Act, under which the Railway Inspectorate still operates, together with a provision for the holding of inquiries into accidents, a practice which had been followed ever since the Inspectorate had been formed in 1840 but which had had no legal basis.

It is somewhat surprising that more parliamentary attention was not devoted to the question of brakes. Thirty years after the opening of the Liverpool & Manchester Railway in 1830 the same rudimentary systems were in use, with just a few hand brakes available, and even by 1870 there had been little real improvement. Whilst poor braking systems were not in themselves the direct cause of accidents, they frequently caused the consequences to be more severe. In 1858 Lt-Col Yolland reported on four brake systems – Newall's, Fay's, Guérin's, and McConnell's.

Newall's brake was a spring-assisted self-acting system which could be operated either from the tender, the brakevan, or from a carriage in any part of the train. It consisted of a revolving shaft placed longitudinally under each coach to operate the brakes. The shafts of up to four adjacent coaches could be coupled together and worked from one position, thus considerably increasing the available brake power. Fay's brake was somewhat similar, but not spring-assisted. Guérin's brake was self-acting, and was applied when the buffers were compressed as soon as the tender brake was applied. However, it did not protect the rear of a train in case of accidental division and was not thought to be suitable for fast trains. The fourth type of brake, McConnell's, consisted of 'sledges' on the locomotive, which were forced down on to the rails by steam pressure. However, if the pressure was too great there was an obvious risk of derailment. Of the four types, Newall's appeared to have the most practical advantages and the East Lancashire Railway, a line rich in steep Pennine gradients, agreed to give it a trial.

Col Yolland's recommendations were years ahead of their time. He said that all express and fast trains should have continuous brakes (not achieved until the 1890s), which should be capable of being applied at a distant signal at danger by a ramp and contact mechanism (not achieved throughout Britain until the 1980s in modified form). In the meantime, he said, the first four coaches on a train should have Newall's brake, worked from the tender, and the last four coaches should have their brakes operated from the brakevan.

Even if those simple recommendations had been adopted a number of serious accidents would have been avoided, such as the one at Helmshore on the Lancashire & Yorkshire Railway just after midnight on 4 September 1860. Helmshore lies towards the top of a 10-mile climb from Bury to Baxenden, much of it steeper than 1 in 100, on the line to Accrington and Colne. Three excursion trains were returning to the East Lancashire cotton towns from Belle Vue, Manchester, with upwards of 2,500 passengers. Helmshore station (now closed) stood on a gradient of 1 in 97, and after the train had been standing there for about a minute a coupling snapped and 17 carriages started to run back down the hill. The guard was on the platform closing doors and he jumped back on the train straight away but the brake on his van was quite useless to stop the runaway coaches, which started to gather speed. Some passengers jumped out in the pitch darkness. Others, afraid to do so, stayed where they were in rapidly-mounting terror as the full realisation of their predicament came upon them. In this instance it was fortunate that the following excursion was close behind. Its driver spotted the tail light of the brakevan coming towards him and he rapidly stopped, providing a solid buffer into which the runaways crashed at about 20mph. Eleven passengers were killed and 77 injured.

Col Yolland was scathing in his condemnation: 'the legislature has not deemed it expedient to entrust the Board of Trade with any power as regards the mode in which traffic shall be conducted, and the Railway Companies have very generally disregarded the recommendations made from time to time by the Board of Trade on the subject of increasing the break power, on the establishment of a communication between guard and driver and on the placing of a break at the tail of every train. The only power available to the Board of Trade is to refuse to sanction any new stations on gradients'.

Even though there were plenty of accidents to occupy the time of the four Inspectors, they were often called upon to consider other matters. In 1863 Col Yolland reported on railway schemes proposed for the metropolis and its suburbs and referred to an earlier Royal Commission report in terms that are peculiarly relevant to the situation today – 'the urgent necessity now generally admitted to exist for relieving the overcrowded streets of some portion of their traffic . . . and the connection of the railways north of the Thames with those south of the Thames'. Although Yolland was an outspoken firebrand, he had enormous prescience. He was referring in the above quotation to the authorisation of the Farringdon-Blackfriars section of line, reopened in 1988 with great success by British Rail under the brand-name 'Thameslink'.

Other arcane matters engaged the attention of the Inspectorate. In 1865 Capt Tyler prepared a report on the Mont Cenis Railway under the Alps, proposed by Messrs Brassey & Co, railway builders, then in 1866 he carried out an inspection of the railways and ports of Italy, with reference to the use of the Italian route for the conveyance of the 'eastern mails'.

Their normal work continued unabated. The promotion and building of railways was still in full swing. In 1864 no fewer than 294 Bills were presented to parliament for 3,099 miles of new line. 1865 was even busier, with 348 Bills for 4,270 miles. Many of these Bills were rejected, and many miles of authorised line were never built. But safety was still the Inspectors' chief concern.

Col Yolland was in action again, following a collision on the LNWR at Walton Junction, near Warrington, on 29 June 1867. The signalman at Walton Junction had shunted an Up coal train out of the way of a following Up Liverpool express by sending it forward on to the Chester line to stand clear of the junction. The Liverpool train approached the facing junction and whistled for the main line at the junction distant signal, which stood at danger, whereupon the signalman immediately cleared all his main line signals. He had, however, omitted to restore the junction points after the coal train had passed over them, and as they were not interlocked with the signals, the points lay for one route (towards Chester) whilst the signals were clear for another (the main line to Crewe). A shunter employed at Walton Junction saw the points wrongly set just before the Liverpool express reached them. 'Oh, my God, Rowson', he called to the signalman, 'them points'. It was too late. The express, with 300 passengers on board, was suddenly diverted from the main line on to the Chester line at 15-20mph and crashed into the back of the stationary coal train. Eight passengers were killed and 70 injured. The poor signalman was sent for trial for manslaughter, but he had Col Yolland's sympathy. The latter was as severe as only he could be in his censure of the powerful LNWR for not having interlocking between the points and signals at such an important and busy junction, despite a recommendation to that effect by Capt Tyler following an accident at the same spot five years earlier. He added that the LNWR would be wise to employ three men on eight-hour shifts at such an arduous post as Walton Junction, instead of requiring two men to work 12 hours. He concluded:

'The utility of their Lordships continuing to maintain the present system of making these unauthorised inquiries into the circumstances connected with the accidents which occur on railways may therefore be fairly questioned, as a stronger instance of its inutility cannot be cited that what has recently occurred with reference to the Walton Junction.'

One feels that Yolland would have clapped the entire LNWR directorate into jail if he had had the power.

The LNWR, very slow to adopt modern safeguards, was to be in trouble several times in the next few years. On 20 August 1868 there occurred the worst accident in the history of railways up to that time, when 31 passengers and two enginemen were killed in a horrifying disaster to the Down daytime Irish Mail on the North Wales coast between Abergele and Llandulas. Whilst a train was being shunted at some sidings at Llysfaen at the top of a gradient, several wagons which had been left on the Down main line started to run back down the hill towards the approaching Irish Mail. Two of them contained 7¾ tons of paraffin in casks. There was a mighty crash as the runaway wagons piled up into the express at a combined speed of 30mph, scattering their deadly contents, which were immediately ignited by the engine fire. The front coaches, and the passengers in them, were consumed. In later years the express would have been saved by throw-off catch points on the gradient, intended to derail away from the main line any runaway vehicles, but such equipment had still to be designed, and would have been inappropriate until passenger trains were equipped with the continuous automatic brake.

The Irish Mail trains were the pride of the London & North Western Railway, bearing in mind that at this time the whole of Ireland was governed from London and the traffic of mails and passengers was very important. The Up train was in trouble at Tamworth on 14 September 1870. The North signalbox had an Up distant signal, an Up outer home signal and an Up inner home. The signalman had set his facing points for the platform loop line as he was expecting a goods train, but when the train arrived it was, to the signalman's consternation, the night-time Irish Mail. The distant and outer home signals were both showing a white light, meaning 'all right', and it was not until the hapless driver saw the junction signal set for the platform loop that he realised that anything was wrong. With wheels screeching on the rails in protest, the Mail took the points at nearly 50mph, ran through the loop and into the siding at the far end. Driver and fireman both hung on grimly as their train rapidly approached the stop block, demolished it at 15mph and plunged into the River Anker. Both men lost their lives and a passenger was killed. There were 11 vehicles on the train, and Fay's brake was in use on the last three. It was better than nothing, but not much, and in any case its use depended upon the breaksman hearing the driver's break-whistle, a most unreliable undertaking.

Capt Tyler inquired into this accident, and came across a situation practically unknown in those days — the North Box signalman declined to make any statement without taking the advice of his solicitor! Tyler made the following recommendations, which encapsulate our theme of 'lock, block and brake':

● Two arms on the distant signal, or the outer home, would have given the driver earlier warning of the way the points were set.
● If a proper block system had been in force the signalman would have known which train to expect.

● A more efficient brake would have enabled the train to stop safely, short of the stop block.

There was a great dislike and distrust of facing points at this time, not without good reason as they could be dangerous without proper locking and interlocking, and caused many serious accidents. This dislike was to affect track layouts until well into the 20th century.

Tyler's comments on the distant signal are very interesting. The idea of having two arms on the signal in order to give the driver advance warning of the way the facing points ahead were set was of great importance and was subsequently adopted on a wide scale. A distant signal with two arms became known as a 'splitting distant', but the practice declined in later years and there was a reversion to the original practice of having only one arm, with the distinction that the arm was only lowered when the junction ahead was set for the higher speed route. There was a great deal of confusion about the role of the distant signal. It was originally designed to protect a train standing at the station (or home) signal in the days before the block system was installed, but it was increasingly coming to be regarded as a repeater signal for the home signal. However, it was regarded as a danger signal, and carried a red light, for the next 50 years.

Up to 1867 most railway companies had adopted the following Rule for distant signals (known as 'auxiliary' signals):

'When a train is stopping at a station, or when there is any obstruction thereat, the main and auxiliary signal must be at Danger, and any coming engine or train must be brought to a stand at the auxiliary signal, when the engineman will open his whistle, and afterwards proceed with caution towards the station.'

Enginemen very frequently failed to carry out the Rule, either because they couldn't see the signal until they were too near to stop at it, given the inefficient brakes in use, or they could see that the line ahead was clear. The railway companies connived at this irregular practice and were censured by the Inspecting Officers whenever it caused or contributed to an accident. The superintendents of the companies therefore agreed to an amendment to the Rule, relieving the driver of the need to stop at the distant signal if he could see the way ahead to be clear. If not, the driver was still expected to stop at the distant signal; only a slight improvement in practical terms. The standard arrangement for semaphore signals was:

● Arm horizontal, red light at night	Danger, Stop
● Arm dropped 45°, green light at night	Caution
● Arm close to the post, white light at night	All right

The Great Western, already showing unmistakable signs of individuality, continued to use disc and crossbar signals, and one or two other railways had their own systems.

1870 was a bad year, both for the LNWR and for the railways as a whole. No fewer than 66 passengers were killed, in several separate accidents. On the LNWR, five passengers were killed and many were injured when a North Eastern Railway goods train ran into the Up Scotch Mail at St Nicholas Crossing, a flat crossing just south of Carlisle. The NER driver was drunk and failed to stop at the stop board. Seven passengers and the driver were killed at Harrow when the 5.00pm express Euston to Liverpool and Manchester crashed into the back of a train of empty wagons in fog. The driver was not keeping a proper lookout, but the signalling system and the operating methods were unsatisfactory.

The worst accident of the year occurred at Stairfoot, on the Manchester, Sheffield & Lincolnshire Railway, on 12 December. Fifteen passengers were killed and 59 injured, when part of a goods train being shunted and made up on the main line at Barnsley ran down an incline and crashed into a stationary train.

But back to Col Yolland. After inquiring into a collision at Brockley Whins on the North Eastern Railway between Sunderland and Gateshead on 6 December 1870, in which five lives were lost and which resulted from the absence of interlocking between points and signals, he tore into the directors of the NER:

'Nothing', he said, 'can more plainly exhibit the entire absence of responsibility that exists on the part of the railway directors, their officers and servants, for the occurrence of preventible disastrous accidents, than what has taken place with reference to this very serious collision, because it appears to me that the company's management is wholly to blame for this accident.

'It is now nearly 15 years since I first called attention to the danger in allowing facing points to be inadvertently moved to the wrong position, and how, by interlocking the points and signals this class of accident might be altogether avoided.'

Had it been left to Col Yolland, he would have tried to persuade the Board of Trade to obtain statutory powers to compel railways to adopt certain safety measures, but that would have to wait for another 20 years. Tyler counselled caution and suggested to a Select Committee in 1870 that if the practice of holding inquiries into accidents were to be legalised, and if reports on such accidents were promptly published, he thought that public opinion would so act upon the companies that 'we shall get all that is required'. He was over-optimistic, but the result was the passing of the Regulation of Railways Act 1871, an important milestone in the holding of inquiries. Its main features are summarised at the end of this chapter.

And so, how did matters stand on 'lock, block and brake' by 1871? The conclusion must be 'not at all well'. Locking of facing points, and the interlocking of points and signals, was proceeding only slowly. The block system, too, was being introduced without any apparent urgency, and some of the systems in use were less than satisfactory. The LNWR, for example, used a system of permissive block which allowed a second train to proceed into an already-occupied section, a bad practice on passenger lines which resulted in several accidents. Little progress had been made on the brake question. All in all, one feels some sympathy for Col Yolland's view, and many more lives were to be needlessly lost before the railways reluctantly came into line. That, however, is the subject of our next chapter.

The Regulation of Railways Act 1871

Sec 3   Empowers the Board of Trade to appoint inspectors:
1   To inspect any railway.
2   To make an inquiry in respect of any railway, or into the cause of a railway accident.

Sec 4   Empowers an inspector:
1   To enter and inspect any railway.
2   To summon railway officers or staff as witnesses.
3   To require answers or returns.
4   To require the production of books, papers and documents.

Sec 5   Additional provisions concerning the inspection of new lines, etc.

Sec 6   Railway companies are to make returns of accidents to the Board of Trade. Certain types of accident must be reported at once.

Sec 7   The Board of Trade may direct an inquiry to be made by an Inspector into the cause of any accident, and may direct that a more formal investigation be held:

1   with the inspector being assisted by a person possessing legal or special knowlege, or
2   by a legally qualified or other person, being assisted by an inspector or other assessor.

A formal investigation shall be held in open court, shall have the powers of a court of summary jurisdiction, and may take statements on oath.

Reports shall be made to the Board of Trade of the causes and circumstances of an accident, and any observations thereon. The report is to be made public.

Sec 9   Railway companies shall prepare statements of capital, traffic and working expenditive.

Statistical Summary 1851-1871

Year	Miles of line open	No of passengers killed in train accidents	No of railway staff killed		No of passengers carried (million)	Freight tonnage (million)	Revenue (£ million)	
			Train accidents	Other causes			Passenger	Freight
1851	6,890	19	64	53	85	—	7	7
1852	7,641	10	57	63	89	—	8	8
1853	7,686	36	62	97	102	—	8	9
1854	8,053	12	39	73	111	—	9	11
1855	8,280	10	28	97	118	—	9	11
1856	8,635	8	30	112	129	—	10	13
1857	9,019	25	18	75	139	—	11	14
1858	9,506	26	17	114	139	—	10	14
1859	10,002	5	14	103	149	—	11	13
1860	10,433	29	17	104	163	—	13	15
1861	10,870	46	22	105	174	94	13	15
1862	11,551	26	20	89	180	94	14	15
1863	12,322	13	11	87	205	101	15	17
1864	12,789	15	15	88	229	110	16	18
1865	13,289	23	28	94	252	111	17	19
1866	13,854	15	17	83	274	124	17	21
1867	14,247	19	15	90	288	135	18	22
1868	n/a	40	19	64	304	n/a	18	22
1869	15,145	17	22	129	312	n/a	19	22
1870	15,537	66	25	90	337	n/a	19	24
1871	15,376	12	18	195	375	169	21	27

Lock, Block and Brake — the Long Road to Victory

Between 1872 and 1889 the railways of Britain underwent a transformation. The mileage of line open increased by over 25%; passenger journeys almost doubled; freight tonnage went up by two-thirds. But despite the railways becoming busier than ever, the average number of passengers killed each year in train accidents went down from 40 in the 1870s to 28 in the 1880s, and indeed declined to single figures in 1885 and 1886; an achievement which illustrates the cumulative effect of the gradual adoption by the railway companies of the interlocking of points and signals, improved braking systems, and the block system of signalling. The number of collisions involving passenger trains decreased from a high of 155 in 1877 to a low of 73, 10 years later.

Such progress was very satisfying to Capt Tyler, appointed Chief Inspecting Officer in 1871, and to the three Inspecting Officers, Col Yolland, Lt-Col Rich and Lt-Col Hutchinson.

Tyler was the first one to leave, in 1877, when, at the request of Mr Westinghouse, he became Chairman of the Westinghouse Brake Co in England. He was replaced by Maj Marindin RE. Col Yolland died in service in 1885 after 31 years, and has the distinction of being the longest-serving Inspecting Officer in the history of the Railway Inspectorate. He had been the scourge of recalcitrant railway companies and his tongue never lost its cutting edge, nor his pen its acid, as we shall see in the succeeding pages. Yolland was not replaced. Perhaps their Lordships at the Board of Trade considered him irreplaceable. Tyler and Yolland made a perfect pair — Tyler unvaryingly courteous; Yolland fiery and outspoken. By the time the latter died it seemed that the battle had been almost won, but new dangers were beginning to appear and there would be new campaigns to be fought.

Col Sir Francis Marindin KCMG
Chief Inspecting Officer: 1895-1900

Francis Arthur Marindin was commissioned as a Second Lieutenant in the Royal Engineers in 1854 and subsequently spent six years abroad, during which he was aide-de-camp to the Governor of Mauritius, whose daughter he

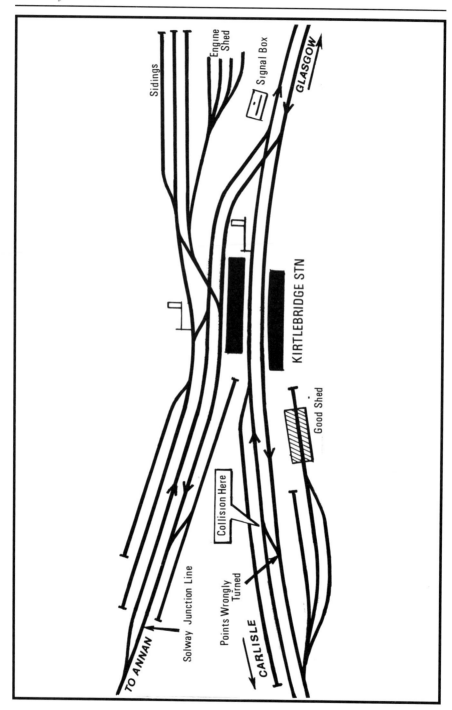

married. He went to the school of Military Engineering at Chatham in 1866, where he remained until 1874, being appointed an Inspector of Railways in 1877.

He was a regular player of football in the RE teams, but was not in the team in 1875 when they won the Football Association Cup. He was president of the FA for several years.

Sir Francis Marindin soon established a reputation in railway circles for untiring industry and unerring judgement, and he performed his duties with never-failing tact and patience. Among his other activities was an investigation into the lighting of London by electricity, and in 1887 he went to Egypt to report on the railways there. Overwork and the effects of the Egyptian climate undermined his health and he never fully recovered.

In 1899 shortly before his death, he gave evidence to the Royal Commission on Accidents to Railway Servants with great force and impartiality, and all his recommendations were adopted and included in the Commission's report, upon which the 1900 Railway Employment (Prevention of Accidents) Act was based.

He died on 21 April 1900 from pneumonia which had resulted from a long day's inspection of new lines a few weeks earlier.

Col Marindin was knighted in 1897, at the time of Queen Victoria's Diamond Jubilee.

However, in 1872, when this chapter starts, matters were very far from perfect, as shown by an accident at Kirtlebridge, on the Caledonian Railway, about eight miles north of Gretna Junction, shortly after 8 o'clock on the morning of 2 October (see sketch). A goods train had arrived with wagons to attach and detach. During this operation it was propelled through the crossover road from the Down line to the Up line in order to shunt wagons in the Up sidings. A short while later the stationmaster saw the train moving back along the Up line towards the crossover, and through a misunderstanding he operated the crossover points to direct the leading wagons across to the Down line. Just as the first wagons reached the Down line the late-running double-headed Scotch express burst into view, coming at 40mph. In the resulting collision 10 passengers and the engine driver were killed. The crossover road and the sidings points were not worked from the signalbox, nor were they interlocked with the signals.

Capt Tyler criticised the larger companies for their tardiness in applying 'lock and block':

'Stationmasters, signalmen and porters must be expected, in the course of their duties and their rough work, to make mistakes of this description. A simple means exists of rendering such mistakes impossible, or harmless. It is to be hoped that this lamentable lesson will produce its effect throughout the country in causing this simple means — of interlocking points and signals — to be more speedily applied over the different systems of railways.'

Several other interesting features emerge from this accident:

- The locking frame at the signalbox was made by a firm that was later to become very well known — McKenzie, Clunes & Holland.
- The block system was not yet in operation.
- The signalmen worked a 12hr day, six days a week, for a wage of 20 shillings.
- Almost all the staff at the station were new and inexperienced, and there was said to be great difficulty in recruiting staff.
- The stationmaster was charged with homicide but acquitted.

The West Coast Night Scotch expresses have figured in accidents throughout their history, and less than a year later, on 2 August 1873, there was to be another, at Wigan, on the LNWR. Under the new powers granted by the 1871 Act, Section 7, a Court of Inquiry, under Capt Tyler assisted by a legal assessor, investigated the accident.

As the 8.0pm 'Tourist' express from Euston to the North, formed of 25 vehicles and double-headed, was approaching Wigan at 1.20am, running at 40mph, several vehicles at the rear were suddenly thrown off the line at a pair of facing points at the south end of the station, resulting in 13 passengers being killed.

The facing points were worked from a nearby signalbox and were interlocked with the Down home signal, which was at 'all-clear' for the express and was not restored to danger until after the accident. Tyler exonerated the signalman from blame, but despite extensive investigation no cause could be found. He suggested that high speeds were undesirable, but in a competitive climate there were strong pressures for speeds to be increased. One benefit of this accident was that the LNWR decided to adopt at all important junctions, where speeds were high, the additional security of the facing-point lock, but facing points continued to be distrusted for many years.

During 1873 and 1874 there were several more Section 7 Courts of Inquiry, usually with Capt Tyler being assisted by a barrister-at-law, Mr W. W. Ravenhill. The LNWR were not impressed by the latter, who soon proved to be out of his depth and annoyed rather than assisted Capt Tyler by pressing impractical questions.

The quest for higher speeds was very much to the fore on the Great Northern Railway in respect of its expresses to and from King's Cross. The company was highly regarded by the Inspectorate for its responsible attitude to safety, and the block system was already in use throughout its main line. However, 1876 proved to be a bad year for the GNR, starting as early as 21 January with the celebrated Abbotts Ripton accident. Another Court of Inquiry was established, with Capt Tyler being assisted by a different barrister-at-law, Mr C. S. L. Bowen. The Inquiry was held in Peterborough Town Hall, and lasted from 24 January to 17 February.

It was snowing hard on 21 January 1876 and a platelayer living at Abbotts Ripton said that he had never known such a night for 20 years. The driver of an Up coal train from Peterborough passed the Abbotts Ripton Up distant and was surprised to find it showing 'all-clear', as he knew that the Up Scotch express could not be far behind and he was expecting to have to shunt out of the way at Abbotts Ripton. He was correct. The signalman told him to set back into the layby, urging him on with the words 'Come on back; look sharp; you are stopping the express'. Hardly were the words out of his mouth when the Up Scotch express burst into sight out of the snow and collided sideways-on with the coal wagons being set back. Wreckage spilled over on to the Down main line.

The coal train driver was dazed by the force of the collision, but he sent his fireman forward to protect the Down line. He next uncoupled his own engine and drove it forward, accompanied by the guard, who was showing a red light from his handlamp. The driver made as much haste as possible because he knew that the 5.30pm express from King's Cross to Leeds was due. Before long, both men saw it approaching at full speed. Its driver saw the red handlamp and heard the explosion of the detonators which the fireman had put down. He immediately whistled for the brakes and reversed his engine but even though he had received the warning as far back as the Down distant signal he was unable to stop in time and ran into the wreckage at about 15mph. Eighteen passengers were killed and 53, plus six members of the train crew, were injured.

The driver of the Up Scotch expresss said that he had seen nothing but white lights (all-clear) at the signals all the way from Peterborough, but when the train passed Wood Walton signalbox, shortly before Abbotts Ripton, the signalman there was horrified because he had not received permission for the express to proceed, and his signal levers were at danger. Sensing that something was wrong, he gave a red light with his handlamp to the driver of the next train, a Manchester to King's Cross express, who fortunately saw it and stopped his train not far from the Abbotts Ripton Up distant signal, which he said 'was showing a clear white light'.

It transpired that the arms of the signals were weighed down by snow to such an extent that they had allowed a white light (all-clear) to be exhibited, and Capt Tyler recommended that the normal position of fixed signals should be 'danger', instead of 'all right', to reduce the possibility of signals sticking 'off' at the all-right position, a practice which was subsequently adopted, but the GNR went a stage further and designed its famous centrally-balanced signal arm.

The fact that the Down express had failed to stop in time in spite of having been given a reasonable degree of warning, naturally incurred Tyler's criticism when he said, quite correctly, that if an adequate brake had been provided, the Down express could have been stopped well clear. Henry Oakley, the General Manager of the Great Northern Railway, averred that he had never heard of a train running past a home signal after it had received a warning at the distant. Subsequently the GNR abandoned the use of a white light to mean 'all clear', and was the pioneer in adopting a green light for that purpose.

Not long afterwards, on 14 April, Capt Tyler inquired into another accident on the Great Northern Railway main line at Corby, on the descent from Stoke Summit to Essendine (the scene of *Mallard's* famous world speed record for a steam locomotive in 1938). In the midst of another severe snowstorm the Up Mail became stuck in a 5ft drift and was run into at low speed, at about 5.20am, by an Up express goods from Manchester to London. There were no serious injuries, but the interesting fact to emerge, in view of the cause of the Abbotts Ripton disaster, was that the arm of the Corby Up distant signal was very nearly stuck in the signal post, and was showing a white light, even though the home signal was at danger. What is more, the same situation applied at the previous signalbox, Burton.

The Great Northern Railway was to be in trouble yet again later that year, on 23 December, at Arlesey Sidings. Owing to the heavy pre-Christmas traffic the 2.45pm express from King's Cross to Manchester and Liverpool was run in two portions. The first portion, consisting of an engine, 13 carriages and two breakvans, was approaching Arlesey Sidings at over 60mph when the driver found the distant signal at danger. He whistled for the guard's brakes, which were applied, but he was unable to stop the train at the home signal, 615yd away, and crashed at 20mph into some derailed wagons a further 283yd along the line, killing himself, his fireman, and four passengers. The driver of the second portion found himself unable to stop at the home signal of the signalbox next in rear — Cadwell — but fortunately without ill-effects. Perhaps Henry Oakley had been ill-advised. Yet again Capt Tyler pointed out the obvious need for better brakes, no doubt with a weary sigh, and he also raised the question of a safety margin beyond the home signal before a train was allowed to approach. He criticised the practice of allowing a train to approach a home signal when the previous train may be standing with its tail lamp just inside the signal, and with a safety margin that was just the thickness of the signal post. Subsequently this safety margin became standardised at a quarter of a mile in the absolute block system.

The term 'absolute' refers to there being only one train in a section between two signalboxes on the same line at the same time, compared to the 'permissive' block system which allows a second train to enter an occupied section after having been cautioned. The permissive system came into widespread use, especially in busy, congested areas in the vicinity of large passenger stations and marshalling yards. The LNWR used it on its main line but eventually had to abandon the practice on lines used by passenger trains and adopt the absolute block system, because there were too many collisions.

The LNWR was concerned at this time about the frequency of collisions in the vicinity of stations, especially where trains were standing just inside the protection of the home signal, and devised a system of cautioning the driver of a second train that the train in front of him was only just inside the home signal at the next signalbox. This was a sensible precaution in view of the feeble braking systems in use, and was the origin of the signalling regulation known as 'Section Clear but Station or Junction Blocked' (Regulation 5), which came into very widespread use but was eventually largely restricted to freight trains.

The railway companies had been unaccountably slow in adopting a better brake, but they professed that they couldn't find one that was suitable. In 1874 a Royal Commission under the Chairmanship of the Duke of Buckingham and Chandos was appointed to inquire into the whole question of the safe working of the railways, and as part of their review they arranged for brake trials to be held near Newark, on the Midland Railway line from Nottingham, in June 1875. Cols Hutchinson and Yolland were present. Eight railway companies participated, and eight different brakes were tested, including the LNWR Clarke and Webb chain brake, the L&YR with Fay's brake, the GNR with Smith's vacuum, and the Midland and the LB&SCR with the Westinghouse brake. The results were inconclusive, with each patentee believing that his own brake was best. A glorious opportunity was lost of standardising on the Westinghouse air brake for Britain's railways, a situation that was not to be achieved until almost a century later. Most of the other brakes failed to meet the Board of Trade's Requirements, issued in 1876, that the brake should operate on all vehicles on the train, that it should be capable of being controlled both by the driver and the guard, and that it should be applied automatically in the event of a train breaking in two.

The 1874 Royal Commission had to consider whether the evidence submitted to it justified giving the Board of Trade greater powers to require railway companies to adopt certain equipment in the interests of greater safety, but they were emphatic that the responsibility for the safety of operation must remain with the railway companies, pointing out that if the Board of Trade had the power to interfere with the working and impose conditions there would be a concurrent transfer of responsibility from the railway companies to the Board. 'We desire to record our decided opinion that any change which would relieve the railway companies from the responsibility which now rests upon them to provide for the safety of their traffic would be undesirable.'

The Board of Trade Requirements mentioned above first saw the light of day in 1858 and were issued as a brief guide to railway companies of the standards that the Railway Inspectorate would require when approving new works. They are reproduced in the Appendix at the end of this chapter and are interesting for their historical importance. The Requirements have been updated at intervals ever since.

The railway companies themselves were busily engaged in improving their working arrangements and several very important Rules and Regulations date from this period. In 1876 the first new Standard Rule Book was adopted by all companies, and specified a fish-tail arm for the distant signal to distinguish it from the home signal. The well known Rules 39a and 55 date from this period. Their observance has avoided many accidents, whilst their non-observance has caused not a few, including some of the most serious. Rule 39a required the signalman to bring a train nearly to a stand at the home signal if the starting signal was at danger, in order to avoid the possibility of the driver's failing to observe the latter. Rule 55 required the guard or fireman to go to the signalbox to remind the signalman of the presence of a train detained on the line owing to a signal being at danger.

The observance of Rule 55 would have avoided a serious accident at Nine Elms Locomotive Junction on 11 September 1880. Maj Marindin inquired into the circumstances. The Locomotive Junction signalbox was extremely busy and was manned by two signalmen and a boy, all working eight-hour shifts. Shortly before 10.0pm a light engine arrived at the signalbox, destined for the adjacent engine shed, but it could not be disposed of immediately. The signalmen changed over at 10.0pm and the existence of the stationary light engine was overlooked. The signals were then cleared for the 10.0pm local passenger train from Waterloo to Hampton Court, a tank engine with nine coaches, which collided at 30mph with the light engine. The leading vehicle, a third-class carriage, was telescoped and broken to pieces. Five passengers and two locomen were killed. The carriages were equipped with Newall's brake but it was not in use. The London & South Western Railway protested that it hadn't yet been able to find a suitable continuous brake. The accident could also have been prevented if track circuits (train detection devices operated by a weak electric current passing through the running rails) had been installed. These were already in use in the United States of America but many years were to pass, and many accidents were to happen, before railway companies in Britain started to install them on a large scale. It was not that the major companies could not afford to do so. On the contrary, they were paying up to seven or eight per cent dividends on their ordinary stock at a time of 'nil' inflation when prices were actually falling.

Capt Tyler left the Railway Inspectorate in 1877 and one of his last inquiries was into a derailment at Morpeth on 25 March. The 10.30pm from Edinburgh to King's Cross became derailed whilst negotiating the sharp left-hand curve just south of the station at a speed of 25mph. Five passengers were killed and 17 injured. On this occasion faulty permanent way was blamed but Capt Tyler commented, with some foresight, 'It would obviously be better if a deviation line could be constructed, to avoid the use of so sharp a curve on a main line'. However, the wealthy and prosperous North Eastern Railway failed to heed his advice, which was a great pity. At the very least, the continued existence of the sharp curve demanded in perpetuity that all fast trains should slow down, and sowed the seeds of some serious derailments in later years.

The Midland Railway was also becoming a force to be reckoned with. It had extended its main line to its Gothic cathedral at St Pancras in 1868 and was now, in 1875, on the point of opening its new route over the northern fells between Settle Junction and Petteril Bridge Junction, on the outskirts of Carlisle. Until this route was opened, the Midland's Scottish traffic had gone via Ingleton, where it was handed over to the rival LNWR. One of the Midland Railway's Ingleton to Leeds 'fast passenger' trains was involved in a collision at Kildwick, between Skipton and Keighley, on 28 August 1875. An excursion train returning from Morecambe, already a popular seaside resort, to Bradford, the wool centre of the world, was stopped at Kildwick because the signalman at the previous signalbox, Cononley, had noticed that its tail lamp was out and had sent seven beats on his telegraph bell to Kildwick, meaning 'Stop and examine train'. The time-interval system of signalling was still in operation, and 5min after the excursion had passed his signalbox the Cononley signalman had placed his signal at caution. This was seen by the driver of the following train, the 10.15pm from Ingleton to Leeds. Its driver next saw the Kildwick distant signal at danger. The Rule required him to 'slow down so as to be able to stop at it, but then proceed if the way ahead is clear'. We have noticed before that this Rule was widely disregarded and the driver of the Ingleton train was no exception. He was travelling too fast to stop when he suddenly came upon the excursion train standing at the home signal, with only the handbrake on the tender and brakevans to help him, and in the resulting collision seven passengers were killed and 39 were injured. The ineffectiveness of the existing braking and signalling systems had again been demonstrated, but the Midland was rapidly adopting the block system of signalling, and had already equipped 627 miles out of 975, with a further 176 miles in process of being equipped. It was also starting to use the Westinghouse air brake, but not quickly enough for Col Yolland, who, upon reporting on a derailment at Wennington, on the Skipton to Lancaster and Carnforth line, on 11 August 1880, in which eight passengers were killed and 23 injured, said:

'If the train had been fitted with a good continuous break it would have stopped before the bridge and saved eight lives. It is all very well for the Midland Railway Company now to plead that they are busily employed in fitting up their passenger trains with continuous breaks, but the necessity for providing more break-power was pointed out by the Board of Trade to all Railway Companies more than 20 years since; and with the exception of a very few Railway Companies that recognised that necessity and acted upon it, it may be truly stated that the principal Railway Companies throughout the Kingdom have resisted the efforts of the Board of Trade to cause them to do what was right, which the latter had no legal power to enforce, and even now some of those Companies are still doing nothing to supply this now generally acknowledged necessity.'

However, the Midland had already adopted the Westinghouse brake for its Anglo-Scottish expresses, but, as so often happens, the new equipment brought new problems. Blea Moor Tunnel, 2,629yd long, lies in a most inhospitable area of bleak and wild moorland, with its southern portal at the head of Ribblesdale and its northern at the head of Dentdale. Throughout the whole of the steam era it was thoroughly disliked by enginemen and track workers alike.

On 19 August 1880 the 3.0pm Down express from Leeds to Carlisle, consisting of engine No 819 and nine carriages, all fitted with the Westinghouse brake, was running through the tunnel (then spelt Bleamoor), at about 40mph, and had almost reached the northern end, when the driver suddenly felt the brakes being applied. The train was brought to a stand about a quarter of a mile inside the tunnel, because the brake hosepipe between the tender and the first carriage had been forced off its mounting by air pressure. However, the train should have been perfectly safe — two more things needed to go wrong before there was a danger of a second train running into the first one. The absolute block system of signalling was in operation, and in addition it was the guard's duty to go back showing a red light, and protect his train. In the event, there were irregularities in the operation of the block system by the signalmen, and the following train, the 10.35am Scotch express from St Pancras, consisting of engine No 1307 and 10 carriages, including Pullman vehicles, also equipped with the Westinghouse brake, was wrongly allowed to enter the tunnel under clear signals, after it had detached the pilot engine. All now depended on the guard of the first train. If he had gone back to protect at once the day would have been saved, but unfortunately he did not do so, and had only gone about

250 to 300yd when he heard the Scotch express approaching. He hurriedly put down detonators, which alerted the driver to the imminent danger. Here the value of the Westinghouse brake was clearly demonstrated. Even in the short distance available the speed of the Scotch express was reduced from 25mph to little more than walking pace by the time of the collision and there were no serious injuries.

Paradoxically, one of the contributory causes of the collision was the failure of the Westinghouse brake on the first train, but the effects of the collision were considerably reduced by the rapid operation of the same brake on the second train. A faulty brass collar had allowed the hose to be blown off its housing, although two years earlier the Westinghouse Co had supplied the Midland Railway with a more satisfactory design of collar. It is a great pity that unnecessary brake failures were allowed to harm the reputation of the Westinghouse brake.

In his report, Maj-Gen Hutchinson recommended that the Midland company should consider modifying its signalling system, to prevent a second train from entering a section before the first train had been proved to have passed through it by the operation of a piece of apparatus at the next signalbox. The Midland did eventually design such an apparatus, the rotary block system (about which more later), but not until there had been more accidents caused by the irregular operation of the block system by signalmen.

Col Yolland's last inquiry took place in January 1885, into the circumstances of a collision on the North Staffordshire Railway near Stoke-on-Trent, between the 9.15am LNWR express from Manchester to Birmingham and a North Staffordshire goods train. There were clear signs that the new era of railway working was at hand but that further refinements were needed. The block system was in operation but the signalman had accepted the express whilst he was still shunting the goods train and he did not have the necessary quarter of a mile overlap clearance. The driver of the express failed to stop at the home signal but because his train was equipped with the vacuum brake the collision took place at low speed and there were no serious injuries to the passengers, although the unfortunate driver paid with his life for his mistake. Col Yolland had just inquired into another collision caused by the signalman giving the 'Train out of Section' bell signal to the previous signalman before the train had cleared the section and he repeated Maj-Gen Hutchinson's recommendation that there should be some apparatus, operated by the train, to prevent the signalman from acting prematurely. As always, Yolland was looking to the future, and thinking of new ways of increasing safety.

The London, Chatham & Dover Railway was not, in the 1880s, one of the more prosperous concerns, in fact its ordinary shareholders were quite accustomed to receiving no dividend at all, or only a very small one, but its signalling arrangements were in advance of those of many a more wealthy company. It, too, was concerned about signalmen giving premature 'Train out of Section' signals and had adopted a system known as Sykes electric block, which contained two valuable safeguards:

1   The starting signal at a signalbox was locked at 'danger' until electrically released by the next signalman.

2   Until the train had passed through the section to the next signalbox and operated a treadle there, that signalman could not send another electrical release to the starting signal at the previous signalbox.

Both Sykes and the LC&DR recognised that the responsibility for safety was passing increasingly to the signalman, and that more would have to be done to guard against potentially dangerous errors on his part. It was at this time that the standard code of block bell signals was formulated, and it came into effect on 5 October 1884. Many of the bell signals have lasted until the present day, although the expression 'Be ready for . . .' has been replaced by 'Is line clear for . . .?' As proof of the longevity of railway traditions, signalmen and others in some parts of the country can still be heard referring to the 'Be ready' signal to this day.

Improvements were now coming thick and fast. The Great Western Railway, although with a good reputation for safety, did not finally decide upon the general adoption of block signalling and interlocking until 1877, whilst the LNWR in 1886 belatedly moved some way towards adopting the automatic vacuum brake. There was still a lack of standardisation in the colour of the lights used in signals at night; red was universally accepted to mean 'danger', but some companies continued to use white for the all-right signals, whilst others used green. Standardisation was important at junctions between different companies.

The worry about the safety of working during fog was becoming a critical issue, and several companies were starting to experiment with audible signals, either electrical or mechanical, as a means of helping drivers, but nothing suitable evolved in those early stages.

In order to obtain an impression of the size and general activities of the railways in the Golden Jubilee year of 1887, it is interesting to compare them with the situation 100 years later in 1987:

	1887	1987
Mileage of line open	19,578	10,345
No of passengers killed in train accidents	25	3
No of railway staff killed	422	32
No of passengers (million)	734	710
Freight traffic (million of tons)	269	125(approx)
No of collisions involving passenger trains	73	20
No of passenger train derailments	49	20

Note the 1887 figures include the whole of Ireland

Today's railway is half as big, carries as many passengers (or more, if season tickets are taken into account) but only half as much freight, and is much safer, especially for the staff. It is also much less prosperous. In 1887 the total revenue was almost double the working expenditure. In 1987-88 BR had to depend on Government support to the tune of £591 million to support its passenger activities, but it is the drop in freight revenue that has been so harmful to BR's financial position.

The two most serious accidents in the 1870s and 1880s, in terms of lives lost, were the Tay Bridge disaster of 1879 and the Armagh accident of 1889. The former, in which 74 or 75 passengers lost their lives, has been too well documented to require any detailed explanation here, but it was noteworthy for the support expressed by Joseph Chamberlain, then President of the Board of Trade, for the Inspecting Officer who had inspected the bridge prior to its opening, Maj-Gen Hutchinson. The bridge had been opened for traffic on 1 June 1878, after great efforts by the East Coast Group of companies, as it considerably shortened the distance from Edinburgh to Dundee and Aberdeen, and strengthened their competitive position. On the night of 28 December 1879 a great storm blew up along the Firth of Tay. The evening North British train from Edinburgh, with 74 or 75 passengers on board according to the ticket collectors, was making its way gingerly across the bridge when observers suddenly saw the lights of the train fall from the bridge and then vanish. The whole central section of the slender bridge, with the train inside its girders, had collapsed into the sea, blown down by the force of the westerly gale. The subsequent Court of Inquiry was held by Col Yolland, W. H. Barlow (President of the Institute of Civil Engineers) and H. C. Rothery (Wreck Commissioner).

When Maj-Gen Hutchinson had inspected the bridge in 1878 it had been tested by using six engines all coupled together. Hutchinson recommended a speed restriction of 25mph and expressed some reservations about the effects of wind when a train was crossing. His fears were not unfounded.

Much public and press criticism was directed at Maj-Gen Hutchinson, but he was cleared of blame by Joseph Chamberlain, who said:

'My Lords desire, in the first place, to state that they have always placed entire confidence in Major-General Hutchinson. No more competent, conscientious, and intelligent officer could be found to whom to entrust the inspection of the structure in question, and they are of opinion that his conduct of that inspection has not been such as to forfeit their confidence.'

He then went on to comment on the perennial question of the extent to which the Government should interfere in the running of the railways, and whether it should have greater powers — questions which are as relevant today as they were then:

'It may appear to some that the present state of things is one which cannot be logically defended and that the Board of Trade ought to be entrusted with further powers. The experience of a great number of years has, however, shown that the present system does not work unsatisfactorily, and a little consideration will show that the public safety and convenience would not be promoted by such a change.

In the first place, if the Board of Trade were to be held responsible for the designs of railway structures and for the supervision of their execution, they must employ a staff as experienced, as numerous, and probably as highly remunerated, as the civil engineers by and under whom these structures are now designed and executed. . . . If any public department were entrusted with the power and the duty of correcting and guaranteeing the designs of those engineers who are responsible for railway structures, the result would be to check and control the enterprise which has done so much for this country, and to substitute for the real responsibility which rests on the railway engineer the unreal and delusive responsibility of a public office . . . to say nothing of the necessary evils of double management.'

The other awful accident of the period occurred near Armagh, on the Great Northern Railway of Ireland, on 12 June 1889. A Sunday school excursion of 15 carriages, packed with almost a thousand passengers, stalled on a steep gradient. The train crew decided to divide the train (a common practice in those days) and take the first five carriages to the top of the gradient, put them into a siding, and return for the others. Unfortunately, the rear 10 carriages were not properly secured and the train was not equipped with the continuous automatic brake. A jerk from the engine during the uncoupling process was sufficient to set them rolling backwards down the hill. The runaway carriages gathered speed, to the mounting terror of their unfortunate occupants. They were unfortunate in more ways than one because the line, which was single, was not being worked on the block system but on the old-fashioned time-interval system. By now another train, lightly loaded, was already making its way up the bank at a good speed. Disaster was inevitable. It was merely a question of how many would be killed. The final death toll was 78, of whom 22 were children, and 260 were injured. It was the worst accident up to that time in the whole 60 years or so of railway history.

   This lamentable affair, caused both by the lack of an automatic continuous brake and the absence of a safe system of signalling, was the last straw so far as the Railway Inspectorate was concerned. For over 20 years they had argued, cajoled, harangued, and used every means at their disposal in an attempt to persuade the railway companies to adopt those valuable safeguards, and by now most had done so. On a number of occasions Col Yolland had pointed out that the Board of Trade had no power to compel railway companies to adopt the automatic continuous brake and the block system of signalling and he had suggested that such powers should be available. Now, although posthumously, his wish was to be granted. Parliamentary and public opinion had been deeply stirred by the vision of all those children horribly killed and mutilated in the Armagh accident and a short Bill was hurriedly introduced, which quickly passed through Parliament and received the Royal Assent. The Act, known as the Regulation of Railways Act 1889, came into force on 30 August and contained the following important provisions:

Sec 1 The Board of Trade may order a railway company:
1   to adopt the block system on passenger lines,
2   to provide for the interlocking of points and signals on passenger lines,
3   to provide, and use, on passenger trains, continuous brakes complying with the following requirements:

- Must be instantaneous in action
- Must be capable of being applied by the driver and the guard
- The brake must be applied automatically in the event of an accidental train division
- The brake must be capable of being applied to every vehicle in the train
- Must be in regular use in daily working
- Must be of durable character and easily maintained

At long last the battle had been won, and within a few years all railway companies complied with the Act. The railways were now approaching the zenith of their importance in the social, business and industrial life of the country and a few facts and figures may help one to appreciate the size and scale of the railway undertakings. The largest, most important, and most prosperous company was, by any standards, undoubtedly the London & North Western, as the table in the Appendix at the end of this chapter shows, whilst the Great Western and the Midland vied for second place, with the North Eastern fourth. In 1889 the total paid-up capital of all the railway companies was £877 million. Total revenue for the year was £78 million and working expenditure was £40 million (52% of total revenue — a proportion which had hardly changed for 20 years). Traffic details were as follows:

Traffic	No of passengers or tons of freight (million)	Revenue (£ million)
First class	30	3
Second class	63	3
Third class	682	20
Season tickets		2
Coal and minerals	212	23
Merchandise	86	17
Livestock		1

These figures reveal two outstanding factors — that the passenger business was overwhelmingly third class and that the coal and minerals business alone was worth almost as much as the entire passenger traffic.

One final point. The term 'block' has been used frequently in relation to block telegraph, block signalling, absolute block, etc. It refers to a system of signalling in which adjacent signalboxes are in communication with each other by telegraph wires, enabling signalling messages to be sent by bell codes and allowing one signalman to operate an indicator in the next signalbox to show whether the section between the two signalboxes is clear on the line concerned. It also incorporates a procedure in which a signalman will not allow a train to pass his signalbox until the man at the next signalbox has given permission for it to proceed. The term 'block' is reputedly derived from the block of wood which was used in early days to hold over the operating handle of the telegraph instrument.

Largest Companies in 1889

Company	Paid-up capital (£ million)	Passenger receipts (£ million)	Freight receipts (£ million)	Ordinary dividend (%)
London & North Western	104	4.5	6.5	7⅜
Midland	83	2.5	5.7	6
Great Western	75	3.8	4.5	6¾
North Eastern	58	2.0	4.7	7¼
Lancashire & Yorkshire	46	1.6	2.5	4½
Great Eastern	44	2.0	1.7	2¾
North British	43	1.1	1.9	3
Caledonian	40	1.1	1.9	4
Great Northern	38	1.6	2.3	5
London & South Western	31	2.1	1.0	6
London, Chatham & Dover	27	0.9	0.3	Nil
Manchester, Sheffield & Lincolnshire	27	0.5	1.4	3
London, Brighton & South Coast	24	1.7	0.6	7
South Eastern	23	1.5	0.5	5

Statistical Summary 1872-1889

Year	Miles of line open	No of passengers killed in train accidents	No of railway staff killed — Train accidents	No of railway staff killed — Other causes	No of passengers carried (million)	Freight tonnage (million)	Revenue (£ million) Passenger	Revenue (£ million) Freight
1872	15,814	24	64	568	423	179	22	29
1873	16,082	40	52	721	455	191	24	32
1874	16,449	86	83	705	478	189	25	32
1875	16,658	18	39	726	507	180	26	33
1876	16,872	38	43	630	534	206	26	34
1877	17,077	11	22	620	550	212	27	34
1878	17,333	24	15	529	565	207	27	34
1879	17,696	75	8	444	563	212	26	33
1880	17,933	28	23	523	604	235	27	36
1881	18,175	23	19	502	623	245	27	36
1882	18,457	18	21	532	655	256	29	38
1883	18,681	11	11	543	684	266	30	39
1884	18,864	31	23	523	695	259	30	38
1885	19,169	6	13	438	697	257	30	37
1886	19,332	8	4	421	726	255	30	36
1887	19,578	25	8	414	734	269	31	37
1888	19,812	11	7	389	742	282	31	39
1889	19,943	88	4	431	775	298	33	41

Memorandum of some of the Requirements of the Inspecting Officer, 1858

At the Stations

Platforms to be not less than 6 feet wide, and when raised, the descent at the ends should be by means of ramps, and not by steps.

Clocks to be provided in a position where they are visible from the line.

Signals and distant signals in each direction to be erected.

The lever handles of switches and signals to be placed in the most convenient position, and to be brought as close together as possible, so as to be under the hand of the person working them. The switches to be provided with double connecting rods.

No Facing Points, except on single lines or at double junctions. In the case of Facing Points at junctions, it is most desirable that the signals should be connected with the points so as to be worked in conjunction with them, and to indicate whether they are open or shut.

Sidings, if falling towards the line, or on a level, to be provided with locked chock blocks, or locked points, leading into a blind siding.

Turntables for engines to be erected at terminal stations.

As Regards the Line Generally

No standing work above the level of the carriage steps to be nearer to the rail than 3 feet 6 inches, where the carriages are not above 7 feet 4 inches in width, outside measurement.

The interval between adjacent lines of rails, and between lines of rails and sidings, must not be less than 6 feet.

When stations occur on, or immediately contiguous to, a viaduct, a parapet wall on each side, 3 feet high, should be built, with a hand railing or a fence on the top sufficient to prevent passengers from falling over the viaduct in the dark.

At all level crossings of turnpike roads or of important public roads, the gates must be so constructed as to be capable of closing across the Railway as well as across the road.

A fixed signal, either attached to the gate or otherwise, to be placed at every level crossing and when the level crossing is so situated that an approaching train cannot be seen for a sufficient distance, distant signals will be required.

Main signals and distant signals for each line are required, at all junctions.

Where the lines are single, an undertaking will be required, to be signed by the Chairman and Secretary of the Company, that the line shall be worked in such a manner that only one engine in steam, or two or more when coupled together and forming part of a train, shall ever be upon the single line, or upon defined portions thereof at one and the same time.

The Golden Age of Railways

In the two decades before Word War 1 the railways reached the zenith of their power and prosperity, and the year 1890, following the Regulation of Railways Act of the previous year, marked a watershed in their progress. They came of age and donned a mantle of respectability. They still continued to grow – from 20,073 miles of line open in 1890 to 23,701 miles in 1914 – but the building of new lines was coming to an end and would have done so even without the upheaval of war and its aftermath. The lines already open became even busier. Between 1890 and 1914 both passenger and freight traffic almost doubled, but the improvement in safety systems already achieved meant that there was no corresponding increase in passenger fatalities, in fact the reverse was the case. In the 10 years 1880-89 no fewer than 249 passengers lost their lives in train accidents; from 1900-09 only 169, and in both 1901 and 1908 not a single passenger was killed in a train accident, remarkable achievements which were not to be repeated for over 40 years, until 1949. Had it not been for a number of disastrous high-speed derailments on curves the position would have shown even greater improvement.

The power and prosperity of the railways reflected the situation of the country as a whole. Britain was still the most powerful nation on earth. Her coal and steel production easily outstripped any other country's, and British steel and capital were used to build railways all over the world. In 1890 UK foreign trade stood at £740 million. Her nearest rivals were Germany – £367 million, France – £311 million and the USA – £320 million. British shipping was pre-eminent on the high seas and the mercantile marine was several times larger than any other nation's. All this industrial activity provided the railways with their prosperity, but it was a two-way process; the country's industrial progress could not have been achieved without the railways, whose tentacles and sinews reached into almost every corner of the land and influenced almost every aspect of life.

This enormous enterprise – the railways of Britain – was watched over on behalf of the travelling population by a small band of Inspecting Officers of the Board of Trade. In 1890 it consisted of Col Rich (Chief), Maj-Gen Hutchinson and Major Marindin. Col Rich retired in 1891, after 30 years' service,

Maj-Gen Hutchinson retired in 1895 after 28 years, whilst Marindin, now Col Sir Francis Marindin, died in service in 1900 of pneumonia, contracted during a long and tiring day's inspection of new lines on the London, Brighton & South Coast Railway. He had been created Knight Commander of the Order of St Michael & St George at Queen Victoria's Diamond Jubilee. It was truly the end of an era. The new Inspecting Officers were:

Major (later Lt-Col) Yorke	1891-1913
Lt-Col Addison	1895-1899
Lt-Col von Donop	1899-1916
Major (later Col) Pringle	1900-1929
Major (later Lt-Col) Druitt	1900-1918

Both Yorke and Pringle were subsequently knighted.

Lt-Col Sir H. Arthur Yorke KCB
Chief Inspecting Officer: 1900-13

Arthur Yorke joined the Royal Engineers in 1866 at the age of 17. His mother was the daughter of Gen Sir Alexander Campbell and his brother was the Fourth Earl of Hardwicke. During his army career he was engaged in the 1879-80 Afghan War and then in the Nile Expedition of 1884-85. He was promoted to Lieutenant-Colonel in 1894.

Yorke joined the Railway Inspectorate in 1891, becoming Chief Inspecting Officer in 1900 on the premature death of Sir Francis Marindin. He was knighted on his retirement in 1913.

Lt-Col P. G. von Donop
Chief Inspecting Officer: 1913-16

Pelham von Donop was the son of Vice-Adm E. P. von Donop, and entered the Royal Military Academy in 1869, obtaining a commission in the Royal Engineers in 1871. His younger brother was also an army man, becoming Maj-Gen Sir Stanley von Donop.

Pelham von Donop was a remarkable sportsman — he was a member of the RE team which won the Football Association Cup in 1875, a fine cricketer (again in 1875, he scored a century in a remarkable game against I Zingari, when the RE team amassed 726 for eight wickets), and he won championships at tennis.

His army career took him to many parts of the British Empire and he was in charge of the Sudan Railways duringt the 1884-86 campaign. He came to the Railway Inspectorate rather later in life than others, not being appointed an Inspector of Railways until 1899 when he was 48 years old. Despite all that had gone before, it was said of him that he now commenced 'what perhaps may be called the most valuable part of his official career'.

He was Chief Inspecting Officer from 1913 to 1916, when he retired at the age of 65. He died five years later.

Col Sir John Wallace Pringle CB
Chief Inspecting Officer: 1916-29

John Pringle, the son of Gen Pringle, was commissioned in the Royal Engineers in 1883. He saw service in India and Burma for six years, then spent two years surveying the Uganda Railway, returning to India for a further five years. He came home in 1898 and was appointed an Inspector of Railways in 1900, becoming Chief Inspecting Officer in 1916, a post he held until 1929.

During the first two years of World War 1 he was Deputy Director of Railway Transport, Home Defences.

John Pringle was made a Companion of the Order of the Bath in 1921 and knighted in 1925.

During the postwar period of Sir John Pringle's service with the Railway Inspectorate the inspecting team was never more than three strong, partly reflecting the reduction in new works inspection duties in the changed economic conditions.

He was chairman of the Railway Electrification Committee set up in 1927 to review the types of electrification that might be permitted on British railways. The Committee recommended the adoption of two types — third rail of 750V dc and overhead of 1,500V dc (with permission to use 3,000V dc in special conditions).

He was also chairman of the Departmental Committee set up in 1928 to consider the extension of the system of automatic train control (now known as the automatic warning system) which had been developed by the Great Western Railway. The Pringle Committee reported in 1930 and recommended the extension of ATC as well as the provision of more powerful signal lights and further controls to prevent signalmen's errors.

Pringle died in 1938 at the age of 75.

As we have seen in the previous chapter, the main requirements of safe signalling and braking systems had been achieved by 1890, but there were still several fundamental flaws in the way in which the railways were operated. In particular, insufficient regard was paid to failures of the human element, and this manifested itself in a number of spectacular accidents in the period under review, from the following causes:

- Drivers wrongly passing signals at 'danger' at high speed.
- Drivers going round curves at too high a speed.
- Signalmen forgetting the presence of a train or light engine standing on the main line near their signalbox.

These three major causes of accident eventually led to the adoption of improved safety systems and equipment but it was a long, slow process, which has hardly been completed even today, a century later, as recent accidents have all too clearly shown. Furthermore, many of the improvements needed were fairly simple and cheap, but were nonetheless resisted by some of the railway companies as though safety were a 'macho' business and the men ought not to be mollycoddled by a variety of protective safety devices.

Some of these points are illustrated by an accident at Norton Fitzwarren at 1.24am on 11 November 1890. A Down goods train had been performing some shunting and was finally set back on to the Up Main line to await a path before proceeding on its journey. The signalman forgot all about it, and when he was offered an Ocean Liner Special from Plymouth to Paddington by the signalman at Victory signalbox, a mile to the west, he not only accepted the train but offered it forward to Silk Mill signalbox 1,500yd to the east, and cleared all his signals for it. The Special, consisting of only two eight-wheeled composite coaches and a brakevan, was coming fast down the favourable grade and crashed head-on into the standing goods train, at a speed of between 50 and 60mph. The 50 passengers on the train had only just landed from the Cape of Good Hope. Ten of them were killed.

The signalman had been at Norton Fitzwarren for no less a time than 27 years. He made a simple human error and forgot about the goods train. Col Rich, in one of his last inquiries, recommended that signalmen should be provided with a device rather like a metal disc, inscribed 'Train Waiting', which could be slipped over the lever of the signal protecting a standing train, to prevent the lever from being pulled over by the signalman in a moment of forgetfulness. It seems such a cheap, simple and effective solution that one wonders why it hadn't been introduced before, but in fact the idea was resisted by many railway companies, who felt that it might cause the signalman to relax his vigilance. Perhaps they were right. Signalmen sometimes didn't bother to use the lever collars even where they were provided, an omission which occasionally had fatal results, but we shall never know how often a collar placed over a lever stopped the signalman from wrongly pulling the signal in a careless moment. This is one of the problems in justifying the provision of safety equipment. One can say how many accidents might have been prevented if such equipment had been in use, but there is no way of saying with any certainty how many accidents have been avoided by its use.

One interesting snippet – the accident reports from about 1888 use the spelling 'brake' instead of 'break'.

The use of Absolute Block Regulation 5 (then known as Clause 16) – 'Section clear but junction blocked', was one of the causes of a serious accident at Esholt Junction on the Midland Railway near Leeds on 9 June 1892, in which five passengers were killed. The signalman there had accepted the 3.7pm passenger train from Leeds to Ilkley under Regulation 5 because he wanted to give precedence over the junction to the 3.10pm Ilkley to Bradford and the 3.15pm North Eastern train from Bradford to Harrogate. The driver of the 3.7pm from Leeds was properly cautioned by the signalman at Apperley Junction, but as the train approached Esholt Junction the driver mistook the signal which had been cleared for the North Eastern train as the one for his own train, and he proceeded past his own signal at danger and ran on to the junction just as the train from Ilkley to Bradford was crossing in front of him. Maj-Gen Hutchinson criticised the use of Regulation 5 at junctions, and such use was subsequently discontinued for passenger trains.

Parliament was seriously concerned at this time about the number of people killed whilst crossing the line at level crossings and the Inspectorate compiled a report showing that in the five years 1888-92, 369 people had been killed, as follows:

On public carriage roads	141
On private or occupation roads	98
On footpaths	106
On footpath and occupation roads combined	24

(By comparison, 64 people were killed whilst crossing the line in the five years 1983-87.)

In their report to the House of Lords the Inspectors detailed the proposals which the Railway Companies had in mind for dealing with the problem, which included the building of a large number of footbridges and a number of road bridges. Under the Railways Clauses Act 1863, the Board of Trade could subsequently require a railway company to erect, at their own cost, a bridge in place of a level crossing, if this appeared necessary for public safety. Level crossings had always been a bone of contention between the railway companies and the public, and continued to be so.

Fog, and the lack of any automatic warning system for drivers, made a potent combination. One of the last inquiries held by Maj-Gen Hutchinson concerned an accident at Castle Hills Junction on the East Coast main line at 3.6am on 4 October 1894. The double-headed first portion of the 10.40pm Edinburgh to King's Cross ran past all the signals at danger at the previous signalbox, Wiske Moor, in fog and failed to slow down at the adverse distant signal at Castle Hills Junction, colliding with an almost stationary mineral train at 40mph. The front part of the express was severely damaged but as fate would have it, no passengers were killed. Eight passengers had been killed in a collision at Thirsk only two years previously when travelling in the second portion of the Up Scotch express, and Hutchinson recommended that the line between Darlington and Thirsk should be 'duplicated' (ie converted from two tracks to four) in view of the heavy traffic. There were no fogsignalmen on duty and the signalman at Wiske Moor had been slow in putting warning detonators on the line at his signalbox. The provision of detonator-placing equipment, worked by a lever in the signalbox, might well have prevented the accident, yet some railway companies were very slow to provide such a valuable safeguard.

Over the decades, both East and West Coast night expresses have been involved in many accidents, and in 1896 it was the turn of the West Coast. Shortly after midnight on 13 August the first portion of the 8.0pm from Euston, the 'Down Highland Express', double-headed by four-coupled engines Nos 2159 *Shark* and 275 *Vulcan*, became totally derailed whilst travelling at 40mph over the curve to the north of Preston station . All except three coaches were damaged beyond repair, but as there were only 15 or 16 passengers on the entire train the death toll was mercifully low, only one passenger losing his life. The speed restriction over the curve was 10mph but it was widely disregarded. Lt-Col Yorke, who inquired into the accident, might have had more to say if he had known how frequently high speed derailments were to occur in the next few years.

Those companies which subsequently formed the Southern Railway in 1923 had been very progressive in adopting specialised block signalling apparatus in order to reduce the risk of accidents caused by signalmen working their equipment incorrectly or irregularly, and the South Eastern Railway had installed W. R. Sykes patent, 'lock and block' electrical interlocking apparatus. It encompassed the following features:

- The starting signal at Box 'A' was locked at 'danger' until released by the signalman at Box 'B' pressing a plunger on his block instrument.
- The starting signal at Box 'A' could not be cleared for a second train until the first train had passed over a treadle ahead of the advance signal.
- The Block Indicator for the section was locked until both home and starting signals had been put back to danger.

The Achilles heel of the system was the need to provide a form of release for the signals in case a fault in the equipment locked them at 'danger', or when a train which had been signalled forward did not proceed. This release took the form of a key, but it was too easy for the signalman to use it without proper thought and this factor led to several fatal accidents, which is a great pity because Sykes' block and the somewhat similar Midland rotary block were a great advance on the ordinary 'free' block in which signalmen could operate their signals and block instruments quite freely, without any interlocking between them. The fatal flaw in the Sykes system was shown in an accident at St John's on 21 March 1898. The 7.45am from Tonbridge to London was standing outside the home signal at St John's in thick fog. The signalman forgot about it and thought that it had passed. When he was offered the 7.0am from Hastings he found that he was unable to give the release to the starting signal at the signalbox in rear, Parks Bridge Junction, and he thereupon jumped to the conclusion that his treadle had failed to operate. He used the release key, which enabled the starting signal at Parks Bridge Junction to be cleared, and the Hastings train entered the section. Its driver expected the section to be clear at least as far as the home signal at St John's and he had little or no warning of the presence of the Tonbridge train. In the ensuing collision three passengers were killed and 20 seriously injured.

The year 1900 saw an accident of great significance. The 1.5pm from Paddington was standing in Slough station, when the signalman at Slough East signalbox was offered the 1.15pm express from Paddington to Falmouth by the signalman at Dolphin signalbox, 1,828yd to the east. As the line through the station was not clear the train was accepted at Regulation 5 – 'section clear but station blocked'. The signalman at Dolphin kept all his signals at danger and prepared to caution the driver of the Falmouth express, but to his consternation the train, hauled by the 7ft 8in single No 3015 *Kennet,* ran by at over 50mph. This would not have mattered unduly if the driver had then made sure that he stopped his train at the Slough East home signal but he failed to do so and collided with the stationary 1.5pm train at 25-30mph, killing five passengers

The Longmoor Military Railway was the temporary home for many Royal Engineers' officers who subsequently became Railway Inspecting Officers at the Department of Transport. WD 2-10-0 *Gordon* is seen at Longmoor Downs during the closing ceremony on 31 October 1969.

Top:

The Maryport and Carlisle Railway was one of the very early railways, and was incorporated in 1837. It had its own booking office on Carlisle Citadel station, as this early LMS photograph shows. A St Pancras to Glasgow St Enoch express stands in Platform 1.

Above:

A detonator, or fog signal. This small device is fixed to the rail head by lead clips, and is exploded by the wheel of a locomotive passing over it.

Right:

Field Marshal Sir J. L. A. Simmons.

Above:
Trap points, in the bottom right-hand of the photograph, are set to prevent any wagons from escaping from the Up lie-by at Witham into the path of the Up 'East Anglian', headed by 'Britannia' Class Pacific No 70040 *Clive of India* on 31 May 1956.

Left:
Capt Sir Henry W. Tyler.

Splitting distants were intended to give advance information to a driver of the route set at the junction ahead. (Market Harborough, Up Main line in 1974).

Goods trains were often in trouble, as seen here at Larbert on the Caledonian Railway in 1869.

Left:
Col Sir Francis Marindin.

Below left:
Great Northern Railway somersault signals at Honnington Junction in 1960. Note that the signal lamps and spectacles are halfway down the post, a not unusual arrangement.

Below:
A fine somersault signal at Bedwas, with GWR pannier tank No 9667 on the 8.30am Newport to Brecon in August 1962.

Above:

The splendour of St Pancras: exterior view, with hardly a private car in sight, probably late 1920s.

Below:

In June 1884 a double-headed Up goods train from Deal ran into the back of a Continental goods train at Sevenoaks on the South Eastern Railway. The remains of pilot engine *Stirling* 0-6-0 No 294 (on its side) and train engine *Cudworth* 0-6-0 No 1 (upright) which was working the train from Deal, are shown here. The Continental goods had stopped to take water. The collision resulted from errors by the signalmen concerned.

Top:
Friars Junction signalbox GWR, between Acton and Old Oak Common, in 1931. On the shelf are the block instruments, bells, and tapper keys for sending signalling messages to the next signalbox. Note the metal discs hanging under the block shelf — these are lever collars, which are slipped over the top of a signal or points lever and prevent the signalman from wrongly operating that lever in a moment of forgetfulness.

Above:
Shortly after 3.00am on 4 October 1894 the double-headed 10.40pm Edinburgh-King's Cross ran past all the signals in fog at Wiske Moor, just north of Northallerton, and crashed into the back of an almost stationary mineral train. This was the result, but astonishingly no passengers were killed.

Above:
The result of the collision at Slough on 16 June 1900, when the 1.15pm express from Paddington to Falmouth ran into the back of the 1.05pm from Paddington. The engine was a 7ft 8in single No 3015 *Kennet*.

Below:
The disastrous effects of the derailment and collision at Aylesbury during the early morning of 23 December 1904. The engine, No 1040, lies on its side on the Down platform. Both enginemen were killed.

Above:
The wreckage of the LSWR Boat Express at Salisbury, after it became derailed at high speed on the sharp curve on 1 July 1906.

RAILWAY SMASH · GRANTHAM 19·9·06

Left:
The pile of wreckage which resulted from the high speed derailment of the 8.45pm express from King's Cross to Edinburgh at Grantham on 19 September 1906.

Top:

Shortly after midnight on 28 August 1907
the driver of the 11.22pm Up Braked
Goods from Tweedmouth to Newcastle
headed by NER 'S' Class 4-6-0 No 2005
ran past Goswick signals at danger and
became derailed when passing through
the Up Main/Up Independent connection
at high speed. The driver and fireman
were both killed.

Above:

Caledonian Railway 'Cardean' Class 4-6-0
No 907, the engine which headed the
local train involved in the collision at
Quintinshill in May 1915, and which was
run into head-on by the troop special.

Top:
Once a common sight on the Midland and LMS — a seemingly endless coal train, double-headed by a pair of 0-6-0s. No 2963 (formerly MR 1195), built by Beyer Peacock in 1876, pilots No 3344 (formerly MR 2067), built by Dübs & Co in 1891 and subsequently rebuilt, near Elstree in MR days. 2963 survived to become 58146 in BR days, and was not withdrawn until 1960.

Above:
In an effort to avoid costly double-heading, the LMS introduced Garratts in 1927. Here, 4992, built by Beyer Peacock in 1930, is seen on a train of empties at Elstree on 5 June 1937.

Left:
Detonator-placers. The pulling over of a lever in the signalbox slides the detonators on to the railhead. The purpose of two detonators is to intensify the sound of the explosion.

Above:
Clearing-up operations at Charfield, following the disastrous collision between the 10.00pm Leeds to Bristol Mail and a goods train on the early morning of 13 October 1928.

Below:
View looking south at Ashchurch on the LMSR Birmingham-Bristol main line on 6 June 1959. Former LMS 2-6-0 No 43017 shunts the stock of the 5.10pm from Birmingham New Street from the Evesham branch platform.

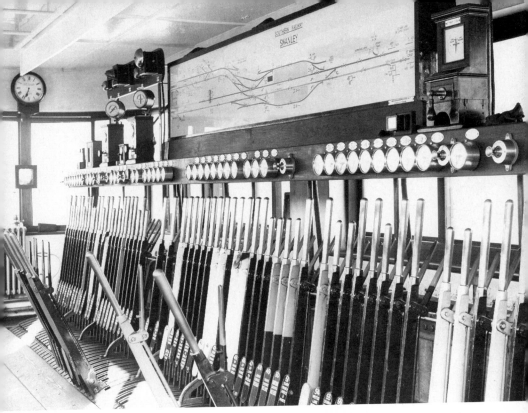

Top:
The Southern invested heavily in the modernisation of signalling in the inter-war years. This photograph shows the interior of the new signalbox at Swanley in June 1939.

Above:
The LMS undertook a major programme to replace semaphore distant signals with colour-light signals in the 1930s. The post was painted black and white to identify the signal as a distant. The use of colour-light signals avoided the need to employ fog signalmen. 'Jubilee' Class 4-6-0 No 45641 *Sandwich* is seen leaving Elstree Tunnel in June 1951 with a Bradford-St Pancras express.

Top:

Culgaith, showing the tunnel and the Down starting signal, together with the modernised level crossing and the now-closed station. This photograph was taken in 1978.

Above:

Leighton Buzzard looking south, with ex-LNW 0-8-0 No 49094 doing a spot of shunting in 1959. The crossovers where the 1931 derailment took place can be seen in the top left-hand of the photograph. The derailed engine came to rest not far from the signalbox.

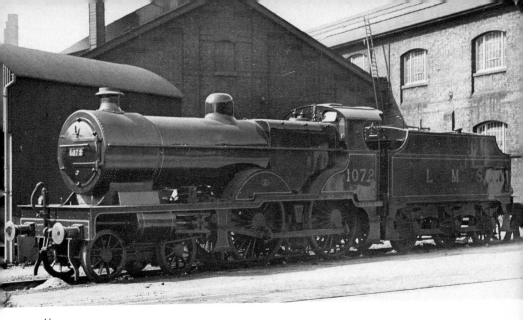

Above:
LMS Standard Compound No 1072, the train engine of the ill-fated 10.00pm Mail Leeds to Bristol involved in the Crich Junction collision of 17 June 1933, seen at Kentish Town later that year after repairs.

Below:
The scene after the collision at Crich Junction on 17 June 1933. Ex-Midland Class 2P 4-4-0 No 522 and Compound No 1072, which double-headed the Mail, await the attention of the breakdown gangs. There are three cranes at work.

Top:
'Patriot' Class 4-6-0 No 5511, surrounded by wrecked wagons, after no fewer than four goods trains were involved in a multiple collision at King's Langley, Hertfordshire, on 13 March 1935.

Above:
The Welwyn Garden City collision of 15 June 1935: breakdown cranes clear up after the crash. It is interesting to note that in 1935 the station was still surrounded by fields.

Above:
No 6007 *King William III* lies forlornly on its side after crashing into the rear portion of a divided goods train near Shrivenham on 15 January 1936. This was one of the Great Western's rare fatal train accidents.

Below:
Castlecary, Scotland, 10 December 1937. LNER Pacific No 2744 *Grand Parade* lies hidden from view in the wreckage after Britain's worst peacetime collision up to that date, when 35 passengers were killed.

Above:

Collision near Hatfield, 26 January 1939:
During a heavy snowstorm, all the telegraph wires were brought down between Welwyn Garden City and Hatfield, and trains were being worked under the time-interval system. No fewer than four passenger trains were standing nose-to-tail at Hatfield, when a fifth train, the 7.15am from Peterborough to King's Cross, came along at too high a speed and crashed into the fourth train. The engine, an almost brand-new V2 2-6-2 No 4813, destroyed the last two vehicles of that train, and one passenger was killed.

Below:

Millions of tons of explosives were carried by rail during World War 2, and one of the very few accidents involving war material occurred at Soham in East Anglia in June 1944. A hot axlebox caused a violent explosion in a train of bombs, resulting in the widespread destruction seen here.

Top:
Directing (or splitting) distant signals at Shipley Bingley Junction. The two left-hand distants were worked from Leeds Junction signalbox, the two right-hand ones from Bradford Junction. Companies varied widely in the extent to which they provided splitting distants. LMS Class 8F 2-8-0 No 48399 is passing with a Leeds to Carnforth coal train on 18 February 1967.

Above:
The Bourne End derailment of 30 September 1945:
Rebuilt 'Royal Scot' No 46156 *The South Wales Borderer* hurries past Bourne End on the West Coast main line with the 11.50am Euston to Workington on 27 August 1955. The junction layout is clearly shown in this photograph, and the tracks from left to right are: Up Slow, Down Slow, Up Fast, Down Fast.

Left:
The engine involved in the Bourne End derailment on 30 September 1945, No 6157, in its unrebuilt form.

Below:
Remarkably, only two passengers were killed in this collision at Potters Bar on 10 February 1946, although there were over a thousand passengers in the three trains involved.

Top:
Faulty permanent way led to this derailment at Polesworth on 21 July 1947 when
Pacific No 6244 *King George VI* came off the road at 65-70mph when hauling the 08.30
express Euston to Liverpool. Lt-Col Wilson concluded that the track was not fit for
traffic of the prevailing speed and weight. Five passengers died.

Above:
Newcastle Central west end in semaphore days. The driver's difficulty in picking out
his own signal on a foggy night at a busy junction like this can be imagined.

Below:

The South Croydon Junction accident of 24 October 1947. This photograph shows the wrecked carriages, in which more passengers died than in any other accident on the Southern Railway.

Bottom:

2-6-0 No 31896 passes Purley Oaks in 1954 with a London to Reading via Redhill service.

Above:

The Goswick derailment of 26 October 1947:
An aerial view of the wrecked coaches, in which 27 passengers and a train attendant
died. The train was crowded and it is astonishing that so many passengers survived.

Above:

Brig. C. A. Langley.

Right:

Col. D. McMullen.

Above:

Pacific No 46251 *City of Nottingham* (the engine of the Up Postal involved in the Winsford collision on 17 April 1948) taking water at Dillicar troughs on a Stephenson Locomotive Society special in 1964.

Below:

The train engine involved in the Blea Moor derailment, rebuilt 'Royal Scot' Class 4-6-0 No 46117 *Welsh Guardsman* sets out from Carlisle for the Midland line with the Up 'Thames-Clyde' in early British Railways days.

Top:
Derailments caused by trains going too fast round speed-restricted curves have punctuated railway history and it was not until the 1970s that special advance warning equipment was installed. Fourteen passengers and three railwaymen were killed when the 12.15pm express from York to Bristol attempted to take the 30mph curve at Sutton Coldfield at between 55 and 60mph, on Sunday 23 January 1955. The train had been diverted from its normal route owing to engineering work.

Above:
Wrecked Great Western carriage after the derailment at Milton on 20 November 1955.

Above:
Trouble on the Southern. The result of a 'Ding-ding and Away' episode. The 12.24pm Staines to Waterloo EMU passed the platform starting signal at danger and collided with a light engine on 9 August 1957. Fortunately, in this instance casualties were light. The driver received the 'All Right' hand signal and failed to observe the platform starting signal.

Below:
LNER Pacific No 60520 *Owen Tudor* lies on its side after running past signals at danger near Welwyn Garden City and colliding with a local train on 7 January 1957.

Left:

ATC (now known as AWS) equipment on the East Coast main line in May 1956. The receiver mounted underneath the front of the engine is passing over the track inductors.

Below:

One of the early automatic half-barrier level crossing installations, at Stallingborough, in June 1962. A Cleethorpes DMU is just about to pass over the crossing.

Above:
Col. J. R. H. Robertson.

Above right:
Lt-Col I. K. A. McNaughton.

Below:
The Scotch Goods in BR days. The Eastern Region was quite content to use its top link engines on 'crack' express freight trains. A4 Pacific No 60030 at Stukeley on 11 September 1959.

Top:
The modernisation of signalling has presented the Inspectorate with new challenges, as the equipment becomes technically more complex and advanced. BR has always been in the forefront among the world's railways in its use of the latest available technology. Seen here is the operating room in Motherwell power signalbox. State-of-the-art signalling has now moved on to video displays and solid-state interlocking instead of large signalling panels and racks of relays.

Above:
The wreckage of the 17.20 express from Liverpool Lime Street to Euston after the collision at Colwich on 19 September 1986. None of the passengers was killed, thanks to the strength of the Mk 3 coaches, despite the collision taking place at 100mph. Maj Peter Olver held the public inquiry into this accident.

The wreckage of the 12.17 EMU from Littlehampton to London Victoria lies strewn down the embankment at Purley on 5 March 1989, after the accident the previous day. The public inquiry was held by Mr Alan Cooksey. The driver had run past a danger signal and this accident finally prompted BR to undertake trials with an automatic train-protection system. The Purley accident will therefore come to be regarded as a landmark in the long quest to improve railway safety.

and seriously injuring 35 more. The driver, who was nearly 60 years old and survived, admitted missing all the signals but could not explain why.

Railway accidents attracted just as much media attention in those days as they do today, and a lot of prominence was given in the press to suggestions that mechanical contrivances were needed, working in conjunction with the semaphore signals, to render it impossible for a driver to pass a signal at 'danger' without becoming aware of it. On the other hand Lt-Col Yorke, who inquired into the accident, thought that it might cause drivers to pay less heed to signals, and he was worried about the reliability of such equipment. Yorke seemed to see all the problems and none of the advantages. He envisaged having the apparatus at every signal and failed to realise the value of having the equipment at distant signals only. It is a pity that he was so lukewarm because he was in a position to give a great impetus to the development of what became known as Automatic Train Control, or ATC for short. Fortunately for the Great Western, a group of its officers recognised the need for ATC at the distant signal and work was started on the development of a suitable system.

The new century, if we consider the year 1901 as marking the start of the 20th century, began very auspiciously. For the first time ever, not a single passenger was killed in a train accident, which was a remarkable tribute both to railway engineers and operators. Bearing in mind the absence of many modern safeguards it could not have been achieved without a very high standard of discipline and devotion to duty, and pride in their particular railway company, by railwaymen of all grades. Nonetheless 1901 saw an accident which had ominous overtones for later years. On 23 December an electric train of the Liverpool Overhead Railway came to a stand with an electrical defect approaching Dingle station on the underground section. Arcing set fire to the train, and fierce flames, fumes and smoke were driven by the wind into the station, which was also consumed by fire. All the passengers were safely evacuated but six railwaymen died in the very rapid spread of the fire once it had gained a hold. Lt-Col Yorke investigated the accident, and in view of the lethal nature of such fires and the speed with which they spread, recommended that as little wood as possible should be used in underground stations on electrified lines.

In 1903 there was yet another collision caused by a signalman forgetting about a light engine standing on the main line near his signalbox. The signalman at Sowerby Bridge No 1 signalbox, L&YR, had let a 2-4-2 tank engine out of the sidings to stand on the Up main line, eventually to proceed via the crossover and the Down main line to the engine shed. It had to be held on the Up line because a goods train was passing on the Down main line. The signalman forgot about the light engine, accepted the 7.10pm express from Leeds to Liverpool on the Up main line and cleared all his signals for it. The express, a 4-4-2 tender engine with six bogie-coaches, came along at full speed, ran headlong into the stationary tank engine, and threw itself across the Down main line, along which the 6.40pm Manchester Victoria to Bradford Exchange, hauled by another 2-4-2 tank engine, was approaching. Fortunately, its driver was alert and saw the signals thrown back against him in sufficient time for him to greatly reduce the speed of his train, and only one passenger was killed.

Maj Druitt inquired into the accident, which happened on 22 October. The signalman was primarily at fault, although the traincrew of the light engine were criticised for not carrying out Rule 55 and reminding the signalman that their engine was standing vulnerably on the main line. Strangely, Druitt made no recommendations as to the use of lever collars or other reminders, nor did he mention track circuits. These had first been installed at St Paul's in 1886, and in 1894 the Great Northern Railway had equipped the lines through Gas Works tunnels. The spread of track circuits into general use was very slow, mainly owing to their cost.

The biggest railway in 1903, in terms of train miles run, was the LNWR, with 47.6 million, but it was very closely challenged for that position by the Midland, with 47.5 million. The Great Western ran 46.6 million, and the North Eastern 30.1.

The year 1904 saw the first of a remarkable series of four high-speed derailments in as many years, which ended as abruptly as it had begun. The cause, or causes, of the accidents remain a mystery to this day, as all four drivers were killed. In two cases the signals were showing all-clear; in the other two they were at danger. The speed in every case was about 60mph.

Lt-Col Yorke inquired into the first one, which took place at Aylesbury, on the Metropolitan and Great Central Joint line, at 3.38am on 23 December. The 2.45am Down GC express from Marylebone was coming fast down the seven mile-long falling gradient from Wendover, mainly at 1 in 117, in dense fog. Its driver should have reduced speed for the curve over the trailing junction with the line from Princes Risborough but he failed to do so, and an exceptionally destructive derailment took place. The engine, four-coupled No 1040, mounted the Down platform, followed by three or four coaches, whilst two coaches came to rest on the Up platform. Sister engine No 1042, heading a Manchester to Marylebone express, came into slight collision with the wreckage, which was described by Yorke as one of the worst cases of the destruction of rolling stock in a derailment that he had ever known. Fortunately the train was mainly run for the conveyance of news and parcels and it had only three passenger coaches, very sparsely occupied by only eight passengers. The driver and fireman of engine No 1040 were both killed, together with two railway servants travelling passenger.

Two years were to elapse before the next case, at Salisbury on the LSWR. The weekly boat express left Plymouth for Waterloo late on the evening of 30 June with five bogie-coaches conveying 43 first-class passengers who had just been landed by company's tender at Stonehouse Pool from the America Line steamship, the ss *New York*. Although the two rival companies, the Great Western and the LSWR, concerned in the Plymouth to London ocean liner traffic would have denied any suggestion of racing to see who could achieve the shortest journey time, there is no doubt that there was great keenness and rivalry between the traincrews and some high speeds were attained. At 1.57am the 'Ocean Liner Express' approached Salisbury at about 60mph, headed by 6ft 7in 4-4-0 No 421. Probably none of its passengers knew anything about the 30mph speed restriction through the station and were therefore not at all worried when the brakes did not go on. The guard was worried but he acted too late to be of any use. The train tore through the station to the amazement of the few staff on duty, but could not hold the rails over the curve at the east end of the station and overturned into a catastrophic derailment, colliding violently with a milk train moving in the opposite direction on the next line. The death toll was the highest for many years; 24 passengers were killed — over half the complement — and four locomen. Maj Pringle inquired into the accident but had no particular recommendations to make, indeed it is difficult to know what he could have suggested that would have avoided such an accident, given the available technology.

The circumstances of the Salisbury accident attracted a great deal of public attention — so many first-class ocean liner passengers meeting their deaths in the middle of the night in a mysterious accident. Imagine, then, the impact on the public imagination of an even more mysterious accident at Grantham less than three months later.

The 8.45pm express from King's Cross to Edinburgh was booked to stop at Grantham at 11.0pm, and consisted of four brake and mail vans, six coaches and sleepers, and two more brakevans, headed by Atlantic locomotive No 276. All the signals were cleared for the train at Grantham South and Grantham Yard signalboxes, but the North box signalman had not cleared any of his signals for the express. His junction facing points were fatally set for the Nottingham branch, over which a 15mph speed restriction applied, as he was anticipating a train from that direction. The signalman at the South signalbox saw the express approach, and suddenly realised, to his concern, that it was going too fast to stop at the station. As the train passed his box, he clearly saw the driver and fireman 'standing looking out of their respective glasses'. The thought of possible derailment did not cross his mind because he was unaware that the junction to the north of the station was set towards the branch. The signalman at the North box was much more concerned. The train swept by his signals at danger and swung off through the junction towards the branch. It was too much to hope that a train travelling at over 50mph could safely negotiate a curve designed only for 15mph. The engine and five coaches plunged to destruction down a bank, then a relatively new hazard manifested itself. All except two vehicles were gas-lit, and fire broke out in the wreckage to add to the horror. Eleven passengers and a Post Office attendant, together with the driver and fireman, were killed.

Lt-Col von Donop, who inquired into the accident, concluded 'It is feared therefore that the primary cause of this accident must for ever remain a mystery'. He also said 'I consider that the accident points, as previous railway accidents have already done, to the unsuitability of gas as an illuminant for railway vehicles'. However, the main cause of the accident was the passing of signals at 'danger', and the express could just as easily have collided with another train as become derailed. It is a pity that von Donop failed to make any recommendation about the provision of apparatus to assist drivers in paying obedience to signals. By now, the Great Western was already conducting trials with its ATC apparatus on the Henley branch. Grantham has gone down in history as a high speed derailment, rather than as a signal passed at danger, even though the driver had no reason to reduce speed for the main line, for which he might well have expected the facing points to be set. But even if he had forgotten about the booked station stop at Grantham he should still have stopped at the signals at the North signalbox.

The last of the four accidents was of a rather similar nature. On 15 October 1907 the 1.20am LNWR express from Crewe, headed by 'Experiment' class 4-6-0 No 2052, approached Shrewsbury at 60mph, passed all the signals at danger at Crewe Bank signalbox and was derailed on the sharp curve beyond. The train of 15 vehicles was almost completely wrecked. Eleven passengers, three Post Office workers and four railway servants were killed. There were about 70 passengers on the train.

The Crewe Junction signalman, on the approach side of the station, had accepted the train from the Crewe Bank signalman at Regulation 5- 'Section Clear but Station Blocked' — because the platform was already occupied. The signalman at Crewe Bank therefore kept all his signals at danger in order to caution the driver, but the train rushed past without any diminution of speed. Nor did the train slacken speed for the danger signals at Crewe Junction. If the train had not become derailed on the curve it would have shot into the station at 60mph and collided with the train standing there, in which case the death toll would probably have been even higher.

Lt-Col Yorke took this inquiry. He considered that the driver may have dozed off, and discussed the possible use of ATC-type equipment, but once again he was lukewarm about the idea — despite the fact that it could have prevented both the Shrewsbury and the Grantham accidents, as well as many others. It is a measure of the public concern at these four accidents that the Rt Hon David Lloyd George was present at the Shrewsbury inquiry in his capacity of President of the Board of Trade.

A significant feature of these four accidents is that they all occurred during the night:

Aylesbury	3.38am
Salisbury	1.57am
Grantham	11.4pm
Shrewsbury	2.8am

Many years later the pattern of derailments on curves was to be repeated:

Lincoln	12.49am	3 June 1962
Morpeth	1.31am	7 May 1969
Paddington	6.11am	23 November 1983
Morpeth	12.40am	24 June 1984

It is a matter of some significance as to how many of the accidents described in this book happened during the night hours, and it is fortunate that most of the trains concerned were lightly loaded. It only serves to emphasise the need to assist drivers to counter the effects of drowsiness or inattention. In the next few years many companies were to experiment with ATC apparatus but World War 1 put paid to most of these developments. It is a great pity that the companies were not given a more positive lead by the Inspectorate. By the time that lead was given the mood had changed and times were harder.

We now need to retrace our steps to the year 1905. On 19 January that year there was a serious accident on the Midland Railway at Cudworth in which there were a number of familiar features:

- It happened during the night (3.37am).
- There was thick fog, with no fogsignalman on duty.
- Signals were passed at danger.
- Nine out of the 12 coaches were subsequently destroyed by fire.
- There was no detonator-placing equipment in the signalboxes.

The trains concerned were the 2.25am Up Mail from Leeds to Sheffield and the Up Scotch Express, which left Leeds at 3.05am for St Pancras. The latter train conveyed three coaches from Edinburgh, six from Glasgow and three from Stranraer, hauled by 4-4-0 No 833 (train engine) and 4-4-0 No 154 (pilot engine). The signalling through Cudworth was rather complex, and there were no fewer than four signalboxes within a distance of a mile. The signalboxes concerned in the accident, and their distances from each other, were:

Carlton Main	
Cudworth North Junction	946yd
Cudworth South Junction	814yd
Cudworth Station North	396yd
Cudworth Station South	374yd
Storr's Mill	1m 484yd

The Up Mail had left Cudworth, and had almost reached Storr's Mill when the Up Scotch express smashed into the back of it. The latter train had run through Cudworth at high speed in the fog, passing eight distant signals and five stop signals all at danger. The first three coaches (the Edinburgh portion) overturned and were knocked to pieces, and the next six were derailed. Five minutes later, fire broke out and destroyed all nine, even though some were electrically lit. The midnight Down express from St Pancras to Carlisle was approaching but fortunately the signalman at Storr's Mill had time to throw his signals to 'danger', and the train had almost stopped before it ran into the wreckage. Five passengers and two railway servants were killed.

All the signalmen had operated their equipment correctly, except that not one of them had placed a warning detonator on the rail, as required by Rule 85 when a signalman was unable to clear his signals in fog. Maj Pringle criticised the Rule as impracticable at busy signalboxes with four lines of way, and indeed the Rule was widely ignored everywhere. He recommended the provision of detonator placers worked from the signalbox by the signalman. It seems incredible that the Midland Railway had not already provided such a cheap and simple safeguard, but it remained unconvinced of its value. Pringle also discussed the question of ATC-type of equipment, but felt that it had not been in use long enough to prove its reliability. He was correct, but it would have

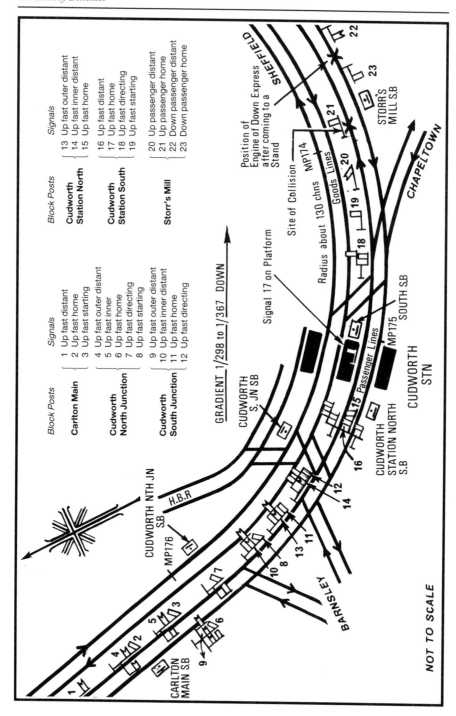

Block Posts   Signals

Carlton Main
- 1 Up fast distant
- 2 Up fast home
- 3 Up fast starting

Cudworth North Junction
- 4 Up fast outer distant
- 5 Up fast inner
- 6 Up fast home
- 7 Up fast directing
- 8 Up fast starting

Cudworth South Junction
- 9 Up fast outer distant
- 10 Up fast inner distant
- 11 Up fast home
- 12 Up fast directing

Block Posts   Signals

Cudworth Station North
- 13 Up fast outer distant
- 14 Up fast inner distant
- 15 Up fast home

Cudworth Station South
- 16 Up fast distant
- 17 Up fast home
- 18 Up fast directing
- 19 Up fast starting

Storr's Mill
- 20 Up passenger distant
- 21 Up passenger home
- 22 Down passenger distant
- 23 Down passenger home

GRADIENT 1/298 to 1/367 DOWN

Signal 17 on Platform

Position of Engine of Down Express after coming to a Stand

Site of Collision

MP174

Goods Lines

Radius about 130 chns

Passenger Lines

MP175

SHEFFIELD

STORR'S MILL S.B

CHAPELTOWN

CUDWORTH S. JN S.B

CUDWORTH STATION NORTH S.B

SOUTH S.B

CUDWORTH STN

CUDWORTH NTH JN S.B

H.B.R

MP176

CARLTON MAIN S.B

BARNSLEY

NOT TO SCALE

been better if he had pressed for the trials to be intensified and speeded up, and had given every encouragement to the venture.

There was a very serious accident the same year on 27 July, at Hall Road, on the L&Y's Liverpool to Southport electrified line, in which 21 passengers were killed. The signalman had run the previous train, which terminated at Hall Road, through facing points into the Middle Road in order to clear the main line. He then forgot to restore the points and when he tried to clear his signals for the next train, the 6.30pm from Liverpool, he found that he could not do so (the locking prevented it). He therefore showed a green flag to the driver, as authority to pass the signal at danger. The driver accelerated his train and was immediately diverted into the siding, smashing into the empty train at 30mph. The leading coach telescoped underneath the rear coach of the standing train. This accident was interesting because there were to be subsequent accidents there, in 1961 and 1977, all caused by an error on the part of the signalman.

1908 was the second year in which no passenger was killed in a train accident, and only one was killed in 1909, which must have done much to tip the balance against heavy expenditure on safety equipment. However, the Midland Railway was in trouble again the following year at Hawes Junction (now Garsdale) during the early morning of Christmas Eve. Hawes Junction in those days was a busy place. Not only did the signalman have the main line to cope with, but he also had to deal with a steady stream of light engines which had piloted trains to Ais Gill and which came to Hawes Junction to be turned on the turntable there before being returned to their home depots. Shortly after 5.00am on a foul night of rain driven by a strong westerly wind the signalman had no fewer than eight light engines in his sidings. The timescale of events at Hawes Junction was then as follows:

5.20am   Engines 448 and 548 for Carlisle were brought from the Back Platform line to stand on the Down main line waiting acceptance from Ais Gill after a Down special express had passed there.

5.21am   The signalman accepted an Up Class A goods from Ais Gill.

5.25am   Engines 247 and 249 for Leeds were brought from the turntable road to the Back Platform line to await a path.

5.26am   The signalman received the 'Train out of Section' bell signal from Ais Gill for the Down special express. He should now have sent the 'Is Line Clear' for the two light engines for Carlisle which were standing on the Down main line, but he had forgotten about them.

5.29am   The Up Class A goods went past.

5.32am   He accepted another Up goods.

5.35am   He accepted from Dent the Down midnight express.

5.43am   The second Up goods went past.

5.43am   He received the 'Train entering section' bell signal from Dent for the Down express, sent 'Is Line Clear' for it to Ais Gill, and having had it accepted, cleared all his signals.

5.43am   The drivers of engines 448 and 548 standing on the Down main line saw the signals clear, and they set off for Carlisle.

5.47am   The Down Midnight express passed, running at 60mph.

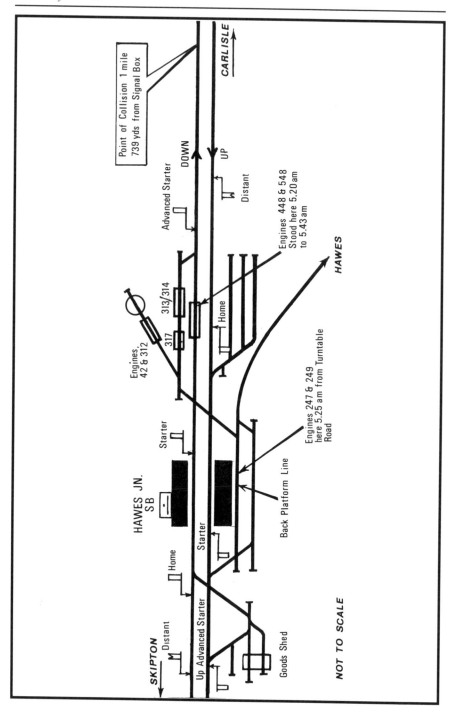

Point of Collision 1 mile
739 yds from Signal Box

CARLISLE

DOWN

UP

Advanced Starter

Distant

Engines 448 & 548
Stood here 5.20am
to 5.43am

313/314

Home

HAWES

Engines,
42 & 312

317

Starter

Engines 247 & 249
here 5.25 am from Turntable
Road

HAWES JN.
SB

Back Platform Line

Starter

Home

SKIPTON

Distant

Up Advanced Starter

Goods Shed

NOT TO SCALE

5.48am   The driver of one of the light engines looked back near Grizedale Crossing about 500 yards north of Moorcock Tunnel and saw the headlights of the Down Express rapidly catching them up. It was too late to do anything. The two light engines had travelled less than 1½ miles.

The Down express, with eight vehicles including two sleeping cars, hauled by 4-4-0 No 549 and piloted by 2-4-0 No 48, crashed into the light engines and fell over on to its side. There was some telescoping between the first and second vehicles, but little other damage, at least until the fire. Within a few minutes a small fire broke out and gained hold quite slowly, but it progressed relentlessly, fed by escaping gas, and eventually consumed almost the entire train, together with the bodies of 12 passengers, some of whom had survived the crash but had been trapped in the wreckage. Maj Pringle, in his report on the accident, said that this was the first time that there had been conclusive evidence of burning gas setting a train on fire, and that since 1868 there had been no case of fire destroying either the lives or bodies of passengers in a railway accident. However, in view of the accidents at Grantham and Cudworth, in both of which fire had broken out, he felt that electric lighting was preferable, but it was to be many years before the use of gas was finally discontinued.

Maj Pringle blamed both the signalman and the drivers of the two light engines for the disaster. The signalman had forgotten about the two engines (a simple human error) but the drivers had failed to carry out Rule 55, even though they had been standing on the main line from just after 5.20am until 5.43am. Admittedly, it was a dirty night; but the fireman of the rear engine should have gone to the signalbox, which was quite nearby, to remind the signalman of the presence of the engines, and the driver should have made sure that the fireman went. There was no excuse for either of them to neglect to carry out such a vital safeguard, but such an omission was not unusual. The Midland Railway still did not provide lever collars to help signalmen, because the company felt that 'They could cause danger if not invariably used'. The signalmen at Hawes Junction sometimes used a poker or piece of wire for the purpose, but incredibly not for light engines, which were the easiest to forget.

Pringle was lukewarm about the use of track circuits, which again was disappointing. He was more concerned about telescoping and had several recommendations to make. His views were reinforced by an accident at Willesden Junction on 5 December the same year, when a signalman's error caused the 8.30am Watford Junction to Broad Street to run into the back of the 8.27am Watford to Euston, which was standing in the station. Telescoping caused five deaths and many serious injuries, even though the accident happened at quite a low speed.

Finally, there were a number of points of incidental interest in the Hawes Junction accident. There were only 56 passengers in the Down midnight express, of whom 17 were in the sleeping cars. The signalbox at Hawes Junction, which is still there today halfway along the Down platform, had been brought into use only six months before the accident, replacing two old signalboxes, and the stationmaster at Hawes Junction, Mr Bunce, had been there for 25 years.

He was still there three years later when, at 3.04am on 2 September 1913, an Up Scotch express overran all the signals at Mallerstang signalbox and crashed into the back of another Up Scotch express, which had stalled short of steam and was standing barely half a mile from Ais Gill summit. Once again fire broke out in the wreckage and 16 passengers died. There were no detonator placers at Mallerstang signalbox and the signalman could only stand by helplessly as the express hurried past under full steam, with the traincrew ignoring his emergency red light.

The first express consisted of three sleeping cars, five coaches and two brake vans, hauled by a '990' class 4-4-0 No 993. It conveyed 13 sleeping-car passengers and 91 ordinary passengers. The second express was a lighter train of two sleepers, three coaches and a brakevan. It was hauled by 4-4-0 No 446.

The driver of the second express had no warning of the standing train ahead of him, other than an anxious shout from his fireman, 'Look out, Sam, there's a red light in front of us'. His engine struck the first express at 30mph, demolished the last vehicle — a bogie brakevan — and buried itself halfway along the next vehicle, a passenger coach, destroying the compartments in the process. All the 16 passengers who died were travelling in this coach.

Many of the coaches were gas-lit and a small fire broke out under the wrecked vehicles at the rear of the first train. However, it was soon extinguished and attention was then directed to rescuing the trapped passengers. About a quarter of an hour later a glow was observed deep down in the wreckage, which rapidly became an uncontrollable fire and consumed the last three vehicles of the first train, together with the bodies of those trapped therein who had been killed in the collision. An impression rapidly gained credence that the fire had been caused by escaping gas but this was not so. It was started by hot coals among the splintered woodwork. Nonetheless that impression has lasted until the present day.

The accident aroused enormous public interest and concern, partly because of its dramatic setting and its similarity with the Hawes Junction collision, barely three miles away, on Christmas Eve 1910, and partly because outbreaks of fire in the wreckage of accidents were becoming commonplace. To some extent they were caused by escaping gas used for lighting purposes, and Maj Pringle strongly urged the railway companies to adopt the use of electricity for illumination. Some had already done so, others had not. There were still over 40,000 gas-lit vehicles, but the number of electrically-lit vehicles was rapidly increasing and had reached nearly 12,000.

Maj Pringle opened his inquiry at Kirkby Stephen in private, that being the usual procedure in cases where there was a likelihood of criminal proceedings being taken against any of the men concerned. However, because of a general public unease that a private inquiry might not be sufficiently thorough, Maj Pringle decided to depart from precedent, therefore the subsequent sittings, which were held in Leeds and London, were conducted in public.

Apart from his recommendations about the use of electricity for illumination, Maj Pringle made a number of other important recommendations:

1   Detonator-placing apparatus should be installed at all signalboxes on main and express routes.

2   All guards' vans on main and express routes should be supplied with coloured flare lights, to be ignited when a train is stopped in section.
3   The construction of coaches should be altered to provide better protection against telescoping and fire. (Telescoping describes the action when the underframe of one coach mounts and is projected along the top of the underframe of the next coach, destroying the compartments and killing or mutilating their occupants in the process.)

Following the Hawes Junction accident the Midland Railway had embarked on an extensive programme of installing track circuits to avoid the need for Rule 55 to be carried out and to safeguard against the possible disastrous consequences of a signalman forgetting a stationary train or light engine. The company had identified over 2,000 places where it intended to install such apparatus. It was also in the process of installing its rotary interlocking block system at many places. This was designed to prevent the signalman at Box A from pulling off his starting signal until the previous train had been proved to have passed through the section to Box B.

Neither of these safeguards would have prevented the Ais Gill collision. Only ATC could do that and the Inspectorate now grasped the nettle. Lt-Col Yorke had retired the previous year and had been knighted as Lt-Col Sir H. Arthur Yorke KCB, and the three remaining Inspectors, Lt-Col von Donop (now the Chief), Lt-Col Druitt and Maj Pringle, produced a memorandum in which they urged the railway companies to carry out combined experiments with different systems of cab signalling and automatic control. It is difficult to understand why they did not wholeheartedly support the Great Western ATC, which had been installed between Paddington and Reading in the years from 1908 and 1910, and was proving very successful.

Finally, in view of recent accidents in Scotland at Paisley and Glasgow Bellgrove, it might be appropriate to mention a similar one at Reading on 17 June 1914. An Up excursion train from Taunton to Windsor was standing in the platform when the fireman thought he saw a green flag being waved. Without looking at the platform starting signal he said 'All right' to the driver, who couldn't see the signal from his side of the footplate. The driver assumed that the fireman would have looked at the signal before saying 'All right', so he started his train and almost immediately came into sidelong collision with the 9.0am Worcester to Paddington express which was passing through at 50mph. Its driver was killed. The platform starting signal had been at danger and the fireman had allowed himself to be misled by the guard's green flag.

The railways reached their apogee in the years before World War 1. It was a position of power and prosperity that they were never to regain. After the war, costs rose enormously and competition from road transport started to be a major factor. In 1913 the paid-up capital of the companies was £1,334 million, and the average rate of interest on their ordinary stock was 4.6%. Traffic figures and receipts were as follows:

Passenger traffic 1913

	Receipts (£ million)	No of originating passengers (million)
First class	4	26.5
Second class	1	12.9
Third class	36	937.0
Workmen's	2	257.0
Seasons	5	—
Mails	1	—
Parcels, etc	9	—

Freight traffic 1913

	Receipts (£ million)	Originating tonnage (million)
Merchandise	33	73
Coal, coke, etc	23	227
Minerals	9	72
Livestock	2	—

Notes:

1 Net revenue in 1913 was £53.3 million.
2 The basis of counting journeys and tonnage was altered after 1912. Before 1913 each railway counted all journeys and tonnage as originating, even though some were taken over at junctions from other companies. From 1913, they were only counted once, at the actual originating point, and this should be borne in mind when comparisons are made with earlier years.

Regional details

	England & Wales	Scotland	Ireland
Length of line open (miles) (1912)	16,223	3,815	3,403
Originating passengers (million) (1913)	1,083	120	30
Originating tonnage (millions of tons) (1913)			
Merchandise	58	11	3.6
Coal, coke etc	191	35	1.3
Minerals	60	11	0.7

Statistical Summary 1890-1914

Year	Miles of line open	No of passengers killed in train accidents	No of railway staff killed		No of passengers carried (million)	Freight tonnage (million)	Revenue (£ million)	
			Train accidents	Other causes			Passenger	Freight
1890	20,073	18	12	487	818	303	34	42
1891	20,191	5	12	537	845	310	35	43
1892	20,325	21	9	525	864	310	36	43
1893	20,646	17	10	450	873	293	36	41
1894	20,908	16	6	473	911	324	36	43
1895	21,174	5	12	430	930	335	37	44
1896	21,277	5	3	444	980	356	39	46
1897	21,433	18	9	501	1,030	374	41	48
1898	21,659	25	16	488	1,063	379	42	49
1899	21,700	14	19	512	1,107	414	44	52
1900	21,855	16	24	559	1,142	423	45	53
1901	22,078	—	8	503	1,172	416	47	53
1902	22,152	6	4	443	1,188	437	47	55
1903	22,435	25	9	446	1,195	444	48	55
1904	22,634	6	7	409	1,199	450	48	55
1905	22,847	39	6	393	1,199	461	49	56
1906	23,063	58	13	425	1,240	489	50	58
1907	23,108	18	13	441	1,259	516	51	61
1908	23,205	—	6	376	1,278	492	52	59
1909	23,280	1	16	318	1,265	500	51	59
1910	23,387	23	9	374	1,307	514	53	61
1911	23,417	14	5	385	1,326	524	54	63
1912	23,441	20	6	337	1,294	520	54	64
1913	23,691	33	8	414	1,455*	568*	57	67
1914	23,701	6	8	417	not available			

* Amended format.

Troubled Years

On 4 August 1914 Britain declared war on the German Empire. That date was a watershed in many aspects of our national life and the effect on the railways was particularly marked. Never again would they reach such heights of power and influence. From the early beginnings of railways until the very day that war was declared their history had been one of continuous expansion and growing traffic levels. All that came to a full stop on 4 August 1914, when the building of new railways ceased overnight, never to be resumed except on a small scale or to serve new developments. When the war ended the railways faced a much bleaker, tougher and troubled future. The cost of labour and materials rose considerably; the railways' virtual monopoly of inland transport was seriously and successfully challenged by road transport, aided by the Government's action in dumping on the market at a cheap price tens of thousands of surplus lorries; and the ability to fight such competition was hampered by the upheavals of grouping, when 120 individual railway companies were forcibly combined into four major groups under the 1921 Railways Act. Then, just as the railways were becoming adjusted to the new conditions of the 1920s, world trade recession developed, which hit the railways' staple traffics — coal and steel — very hard.

Almost immediately upon the outbreak of war, in fact on the second day, the Government took control of the railways in Britain, and did not relinquish that control until 31 August 1919. The three years after 1919 were spent preparing for what today would be called the 'Big Bang' — the grouping, which came into effect on 1 January 1923 and produced the 'Big Four': the London Midland & Scottish Railway, the London & North Eastern Railway, the Great Western Railway and the Southern Railway.

The LMS was by far the largest and whilst the three other groups were reasonably logical and felicitous it is interesting to speculate on other possible permutations, such as a fifth group composed of the Midland, the Great Central and the Glasgow and South Western, which would have resulted in five groups of more equal size.

At the end of 1922, railway capital amounted to £1,174 million. Nett income was £54.5 million and the average dividend for the year on ordinary shares was

4.62%. The results of the largest four pre-grouping companies for 1922 were (£ million):

	Authorised capital	Ordinary share dividend	Passenger receipts	Freight receipts
LNWR	£202	8½%	£19.1	£22.8
Midland	£205	6%	£9.1	£16.2
GWR	£149	8%	£14.7	£18.8
NER	£101	7½%	£6.8	£12.7

The Big Four took over 24,319 steam and electric locomotives, 51,570 passenger-carrying vehicles, 722,639 goods vehicles and 678,105 staff (including 71,440 drivers and firemen, and 24,074 guards). (There were also approximately 630,000 privately-owned wagons.)

Finally, in this statistical survey, the results of the Big Four for their first year were (£ million):

	Total capital	Passenger receipts	Freight receipts
LMS	£415	£32.6	£46.2
LNER	£318	£22.0	£36.2
GWR	£161	£13.8	£18.1
SR	£144	£17.3	£6.1

Within the Inspectorate there was also some change. Lt-Col von Donop retired in 1916, after 17 years' service, and Lt-Col Druitt in 1918, after 18 years, to be replaced by Maj (later Lt-Col) Hall 1919-1927 and Maj Mount (later Lt-Col Sir Alan Mount) 1919-1949. The father of the Inspectorate during this period was Col Sir John Pringle (knighted in 1925), who had joined the service at the turn of the century, became Chief Inspecting Officer in 1916 and remained until 1929. The Inspectorate was transferred from the Board of Trade in 1919 upon the formation of the Ministry of Transport but its duties, rights and responsibilities were unchanged.

Lt-Col Sir Alan Mount CB, CBE
Chief Inspecting Officer: 1929-49

Alan Mount was commissioned in the Royal Engineers at the age of 20, and after training he was sent to India and appointed Assistant Engineer on the North Western Railway. In 1911 he was in charge of the construction of the Delhi Durbar light railway system, and on the outbreak of war in 1914 he went to France, becoming finally Deputy Chief Engineer Railways, for which service he was awarded the Legion of Honour in 1917.

In 1919 he accepted an appointment as an Inspecting Officer of Railways, becoming chief in 1929, a post which he held for a further 20 years until his retirement in 1949.

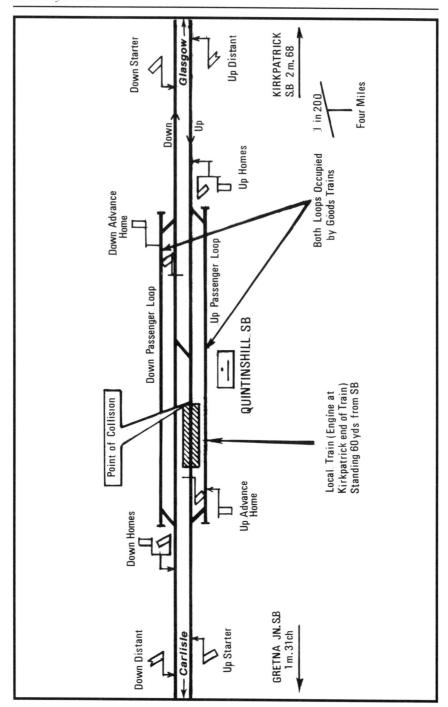

In 1938 he went to India accompanied by W. A. Stanier of the LMSR. At the request of the Indian Railway Board, Mount went to serve as Chairman of a special committee to investigate the unexplained serious derailments of some new Pacific-type locomotives. He was made a Commander of the British Empire in 1919, Companion of the Order of the Bath in 1931, and received a Knighthood in 1941.

During World War 2 the Inspectorate, under Sir Alan's guidance, was responsible for sanctioning and supervising the expenditure of some £100 million by the railways on additional works needed to meet the very heavy wartime commitments. These works included arrangements for closing certain London tubes in emergency to prevent flooding from bomb damage.

A strong advocate of ATC, he persuaded the Railway Executive on its formation to plan for its extension to all main line routes, though the system finally adopted was the inductive type instead of the mechanical contact type in use on the GWR. At the same time, largely as a result of his advocacy, the Railway Executive decided to embark on an extensive programme for the installation of safety devices to assist signalmen, such as track circuits to control signals and block instruments.

During World War 2 and its aftermath, the workload and responsibilities of the Chief Inspecting Officer were very heavy, and shortly after retirement his health broke down, due mainly to continual overwork and he died in 1955. He was a man of great charm.

What were the major preoccupations of the Inspectorate and the Big Four in 1923, so far as safety was concerned? The three main ones continued to be:

- The need to do more to help the driver in his obedience of signals, especially during fog and darkness.
- The need to do more, by the increased use of technical equipment, to prevent errors by signalmen.
- The need for stronger coaches, and the elimination of gas-lighting.

Although wartime conditions, and their aftermath, were not representative in many respects, and will not therefore be considered in our story, there were two accidents which must be mentioned because they illustrate so clearly the typical dangers of the times. The first was at Quintinshill, near Gretna, and happened on Saturday 22 May 1915. Quintinshill lies 10 miles north of Carlisle, on the Caledonian Railway main line to Glasgow, between the signalboxes at Gretna Junction (1m 31ch to the south) and Kirkpatrick (2m 68ch to the north). There were Up and Down passenger loops.

The 6.10am local passenger train from Carlisle, consisting of 4-6-0 No 907 and four vehicles, had to be shunted at Quintinshill out of the way of the midnight express from Euston to Glasgow, which was close behind. As the Down passenger loop was occupied, the signalman decided to back the train through the crossover to stand on the Up main line.

Obviously, the local would have been in a very vulnerable position standing exposed on the main line, therefore a number of safeguards had been devised to meet such an eventuality. These were:

● Rule 55. It was the fireman's duty to go to the signalbox to remind the signalman of the presence of the train, and to stay there as a continuing reminder unless the signalman gave an assurance that he had taken protective measures. The fireman went to the signalbox but he left without that vital assurance, a not uncommon occurrence then or since.

● The signalman did not give that vital assurance because in fact he had not taken, and did not take, any protective measures. He failed to place a lever collar over the Up home signal lever (collars were provided at Quintinshill, but the signalmen only bothered to use them when the loops were blocked with stabled wagons, thus confirming the views of those companies which had resisted the use of lever collars on the grounds that they could be counter-productive unless they were always used. Companies feared that the provision of lever collars might cause signalmen to be less vigilant and the use of lever collars by signalmen has always been somewhat sporadic). The signalman should also have sent the 'Blocking Back' bell signal to Kirkpatrick and placed his Up main block indicator to 'Train on Line'. This would have informed the Kirkpatrick signalman not to offer another train to Quintinshill and would have reminded the signalman at the latter box not to accept one. Unfortunately, at the time, the block indicator was already at 'Train on line' for an empty wagon train which was making its way into the Up loop. When it was clear inside, one of the signalmen gave 'Train out of Section' to Kirkpatrick but failed to follow it up with the 'Blocking Back' signal. Kirkpatrick thereupon offered another train, a troop special, which was immediately, and wrongly, accepted by Quintinshill, in contravention of the Block Regulations, because the local train was standing on the same line just outside the signalbox. The signalman had forgotten about it.

The stage was thus set for disaster. All the signals were cleared for the troop special, of 15 coaches and six vans, conveying the 1/7 Royal Scots, which was coming fast down the favourable gradient. At the same time, approaching from the south, was the Scotch express, double-headed with 13 coaches.

As the last fateful seconds ticked away the two signalmen carried on completely unaware of impending doom. The night shift man was reading the paper and the early turn man was busy completing the train register book (TRB). The signalmen should have changed over at 6.0am but the early turn man travelled on the local train and so did not arrive until 6.30am. To avoid being discovered doing this, which was against the Rules, the night man made all the TRB entries after 6.00am on a piece of paper, to be copied later into the TRB by the early turn signalman in his own handwriting. It was not an uncommon practice throughout the railways, and the authorities knew all about it, but pretended not to. Both parties therefore took part in one of those elaborate charades that are part and parcel of everyday employee/supervisor relationship on the railway. It was always an unnecessary charade, and it distracted the early turn signalman at a critical moment.

At 6.40am the troop train crashed at full speed into the engine of the local train with great force. Moments later the Scotch express ploughed into the wreckage, also at full speed. The old wooden coaches in the troop train were smashed to pieces, and fire broke out, fed by gas from the tanks underneath the coaches. 215 troops were killed in the special, seven passengers in the express and two in the local. It was Britain's worst ever rail disaster, and was caused, said Lt-Col Druitt, who held a public inquiry into the accident, by the inexcusable carelessness and inattention to duty of the two signalmen. He did not blame the Caledonian Railway for not installing track circuits there, although they would have prevented the accident. Perhaps there was not as much recognition in those days of the need to guard against human error or carelessness. Track circuits were subsequently installed on a very wide scale and have done much to improve safety.

Once again the Inspector condemned the use of gas for lighting carriages and urged the use of steel in their construction, both for greater strength and to reduce the fire risk. He considered that the fire was started by live coals in the wooden wreckage and was then intensified by the escaping gas; and he was of the opinion that the wreckage would have been destroyed by fire even if the carriages had been electrically-lit.

Later the same year, at St Bede's Junction NER, there was a serious collision between the 7.5am passenger train from South Shields to Newcastle and a light engine. The first two coaches, both gas-lit, were telescoped and caught fire. Eighteen passengers were killed. Lt-Col von Donop, in one of his last inquiries, found that the cause of the accident was an error by the signalman, compounded by a delay by the fireman in carrying out Rule 55.

However, apart from these two accidents, the safety record during the remainder of the war and its aftermath was not at all a bad one. Only 55 passengers were killed in train accidents between 1916 and 1922, an average of only eight per year, but the new era of the Big Four started ominously. At 5.6am on 13 February 1923 the Up Aberdeen sleeper passed all signals at danger at Retford and collided with a goods train at 60mph, killing the driver, fireman and a locomotive inspector. The express was headed by Atlantic No 298 and consisted of 11 vehicles, all electrically-lit. Lt-Col Pringle considered that the absence of passenger fatalities was due to the use of buckeye couplings and Pullman-type gangways. There were no detonator-placers in the signalbox and they might have prevented the collision. Pringle recommended that they should be provided 'pending ATC', from which remark it seems clear that he expected ATC to be installed on the East Coast main line within the next few years. Little did he know that it was to be nearly 40 years before that happened.

Drivers' and signalmen's errors continued to plague the railways. Five passengers were killed on 26 April 1924, when the 7.15am electric multiple-unit from Watford to Euston ran into the back of the 5.30am Cup Final special excursion from Coventry which was standing at Euston No 4 Up Slow home signal. The signalman had sent 'Train out of Section' for the Up Slow line in error for the Up Fast and had accepted the Watford EMU, clearing all his signals for it. All the coaches of the special excursion were gas-lit but fortunately there was no fire. Lt Col Pringle said quite correctly that the accident would have been prevented by track circuits, but he didn't see a special case for their installation at that location. He might also have said that 'lock and block' equipment, with the treadle beyond the home signal, would have prevented it. The LMS did not adopt the Midland's rotary block.

Both the driver and signalman were at fault in an accident at Haymarket on 28 July 1924, which the 'lock and block' system in use there failed to prevent. The 6.54pm Edinburgh Waverley to Kirkliston ran into the 6.41pm Inner Circle train which was standing at the Down Slow platform. Even though the collision took place at only 10mph, telescoping took place and five passengers were killed. The signalman had not properly carried out Rule 40(a) at Princes Street Gardens, in that he had not brought the Kirkliston train quite or nearly to a stand at his home signal before lowering it, even though his starting signal was still at danger. The driver was misled and passed the starting signal in error. There were significantly no detonator placers at Princes Street Gardens; their use might well have prevented the collision. It is odd that the railway companies were so dilatory in providing such useful yet cheap equipment and it is difficult to understand why this was so. Nor did the Inspectorate press the issue as hard as they might have done and one cannot escape the feeling that both the Inspectorate and the railway companies were perhaps in a state of some complacency over the admittedly good safety record, helped by the excellent result in 1925, when not a single passenger was killed in a train accident on the main line railways (one was killed at Baker Street station Metropolitan Railway). Indeed, Sir John Pringle, knighted that year, was sufficiently moved to remark, somewhat rashly in view of later events, that the case for the adoption of ATC was less urgent and that the expenditure which would be incurred could not be justified at the present moment.

Level crossings had always been a source of concern, with many deaths of pedestrians and road users each year, but because they were mainly the result of the user's own lack of care little was done to make them safer. There had been a few derailments and some passenger deaths, but as long as a big heavy locomotive could generally be expected to brush to one side a light road vehicle the railways were satisfied to leave things as they were. One of the more serious accidents in which the train fared the better occurred at Naworth, between Low Row and Brampton, on the Newcastle to Carlisle line, on 30 August 1926. The level crossing, on a minor road, was protected by distant and stop signals, but they were not interlocked with the gates, which were thus free to be opened at any time. The gatekeeper, who was also the porter at the station, was provided with repeater indicators of the block instruments for the section, so that he could tell when a train was coming. Just after lunch an open 26hp charabanc, with five transverse seats, approached the level crossing. The porter, fatally, did not look at the block indicators nor did he put the signals to danger, but straightaway opened the gates. The vehicle moved on to the level crossing at no more than walking pace just as the 1.18pm express from Newcastle to Carlisle swept through the station at 50mph. The locomotive, 4-4-0 No 1029, demolished the charabanc, killing eight of its passengers. The porter himself was also killed. It transpired that the signals were not always put back to 'danger' when the gates were opened, and Lt-Col Mount recommended that they should be interlocked with the gates. Naworth was a quiet little station, handling no more than 15 passengers and eight milk cans a day.

The Midland main line north of Sheffield was somewhat busier in those days than it is today, with a constant procession of long, ponderous freight trains, usually double-headed, on the slow lines. A 7.20am special from Westhouses to Royston, with 90 wagons of coal double-headed by 0-6-0 No 3980 and 2-4-0 No 270, was crawling along the Down Slow line when the drawbar of a wagon near the front of the train, a 23-year old 10-ton Hickleton Main Colliery wagon, was pulled out and the wagon became derailed. The driver braked when he saw what had happened, but although he was travelling at little more than walking pace the following wagons piled up into derailment. The 10.10am York to Bristol express, headed by Class 2P 4-4-0 No 387 and carrying 70 passengers, was just passing at the time and the wreckage ripped out the sides and interior of the last two coaches, killing nine of the passengers. An empty wagon train which was passing along the Up Slow line at the same time had several of its 81 wagons derailed. This train was headed by an elderly 0-6-0 No 2537 and a 4-4-0 No 303. The site of the accident, which happened on 19 November 1926, was about a quarter of a mile south of Parkgate and Rawmarsh station. The accident was rank bad luck and there was little that Col Sir John Pringle could recommend, other than improved wagon maintenance.

A more common type of accident occurred on 24 November that year between Barking and Dagenham on the London, Tilbury & Southend section of the LMS. In dense fog the 6.17pm Fenchurch Street to Shoeburyness passed all the signals at danger at Upney (the driver admitted that he did not see them) and crashed into the 6.07pm Fenchurch Street to Southend, which was running slowly and preparing to stop at Gate Street home signals. No fewer than 404 passengers complained of injury (a record) but only four were actually sent to hospital. There was no fogsignalman at Upney's distant signal and the 6.17pm train should not have been allowed to proceed to Upney. Worse still, there were no detonator placers at Upney and the signalman had failed to place a detonator on the line by hand. It was a disgraceful state of affairs, which eventually led the LMS to consider equipping the line with ATC, as fog was so prevalent.

The year 1928 caused the prevailing complacency to be rudely disturbed. No fewer than 48 passengers lost their lives that year in six separate accidents, and 275 were injured; the worst peacetime year since 1906. Two accidents call for special comment.

Wamphray was a small signalbox between Dinwoodie and Beattock, at the end of the 35 miles of easy gradients from Carlisle. The signalman had received 'Train entering Section' for a Down freight train, then he dozed off. Waking with a start he jumped to the conclusion that the freight train must have passed so he gave 'Train out of Section' to the signalman at Dinwoodie and was immediately offered the 7.30pm 'Royal Highlander' from Euston to Aberdeen and Inverness, double-headed by 4-4-0s No 14435 and Standard Compound No 1176, and 12 coaches. He accepted the express and shortly afterwards received the 'Train entering Section' signal. It was just before 3.00am on 25 October 1928. The express was running easily, at over 60mph, when

85

suddenly the pilot engine driver caught sight of the tail lights of the freight train ahead. It had not passed clear of the section after all, but had failed with an engine defect. In the ensuing collision all four locomen were killed when their engines overturned down an embankment, but partly because their train was lightly loaded there were no passenger deaths.

Lt-Col Mount criticised the guard of the freight train for not carrying out protection quickly enough — the freight train had been standing for 15min — and he resurrected the old idea of the flare or Very light, which might have given more timely warning to the unfortunate locomen of the express. He was silent about the benefits of 'lock and block', which would have prevented the accident on this main line.

A more serious collision, in terms of its consequences, had happened less than a fortnight earlier, on 13 October at Charfield, a small wayside station on the former Midland Railway's Birmingham to Bristol line. It was Col Sir John Pringle's last public inquiry and its particular characteristics must have seemed very familiar to him by now. The signalman at Charfield was working to Berkeley Road Junction signalbox to the north (4¾ miles) and Wickwar to the south (2 miles). He had accepted the 9.15pm GWR fitted freight train Oxley Sidings, Wolverhampton, to Bristol and had decided to shunt it clear of the main line for the following train to pass, by setting it back into the Down lie bye. The freight train, consisting of 49 loaded wagons, headed by 2-6-0 No 6381, arrived at 5.15am and was slowly propelled into the lie bye. A minute later the signalman accepted the 10.00pm Leeds to Bristol Down mail and passenger train from Berkeley Road Junction and received 'Train entering Section' for it at 5.16am. He was quite in order in accepting the Mail because he had an outer home signal 440yd in rear of his inner home, which had been specially provided to allow him to accept trains when the line beyond the inner home signal was still occupied.

In the meantime he had accepted an empty wagon train on the Up Main line from Wickwar and had received the 'Train entering Section' signal for it at 5.13am. The signalman was anxiously watching the progress of the GWR freight train setting back because he knew that the Mail was closely approaching and he feared that it might be delayed. The thought that the Mail might run past his signals at danger never entered his head. Why should it have done?

The Mail consisted of 11 vehicles, hauled by Class 3P 4-4-0 No 714, marshalled as follows:

6-wheeled parcel van	Gas-lit
6-wheeled van	Electric
12-wheeled composite coach	Gas
Two Corridor Thirds	Gas
Corridor composite	Electric
Four Post Office vans	Gas
Bogie brakevan	Electric

The train was not one of the LMS's crack expresses and was mainly run for the conveyance of mails. The passenger coaches were between 19 and 29 years old and three out of the four were gas-lit. There were about 60 passengers on the train.

The signalman saw the track circuit indicator at the outer home signal move from 'Clear' to 'Occupied', which told him that the Mail had arrived, but then he was somewhat taken aback to see it return to 'Clear'. Was it possible, he thought to himself, that the Mail had run past his signal? No, it couldn't be. It must be the indicator playing up. He glanced again to see whether the GW freight had got clear inside. The engine was still on the main line but he reckoned that within a few moments it would be inside and he would be able to restore his points and clear his signals for the Mail, but whilst he was idly musing on this he suddenly saw through the over-bridge by the points a flash of light, and he heard the sound of a collision. The freight train engine was still on the main line, when the Mail engine hit it and bounced off into the empty wagon train which was just passing on the Up Main line. The two engines and some wrecked wagons virtually blocked the way beyond the bridge. The Mail's coaches had nowhere to go and so they piled themselves up on each side of, and under, the bridge in an inextricable mass of steel work and smashed timber. Fire started in the wreckage and rapidly grew into a furnace, with the result that the first seven vehicles of the Mail were completely burnt out.

Sixteen passengers were killed and 24 were injured; more than half the complement. Thirteen GPO sorters and four traincrew members were also injured.

Sir John Pringle set to work to investigate the cause of the accident, amid intense public interest and speculation. The position of Charfield's Down distant was the key question. Was it 'On' (danger) or 'Off' (clear)? According to the signalling equipment and interlocking it must have been On. The driver of the GWR goods train had clearly seen it showing a full red light only a few minutes earlier. The Mail driver had also seen it clearly and claimed that it was showing a green light. The fireman said that he also saw it at Clear. 'He's got it Off, mate', he had said to the driver. He confirmed that it was showing a full green light. Half an hour after the accident the Mail driver went to the signalbox and said to the signalman 'The Down distant was Off when I passed it'.

'Impossible', replied the signalman.

Sir John was faced with contradictory evidence but he came to the only possible conclusion based on the evidence — that the Mail train driver had passed the Down distant signal in the danger (warning) position, and thereafter passed the down outer and inner home signals at danger. The jury at the coroner's inquest were unanimously of the opinion that the collision was caused by the negligence of the driver in passing his signals at danger. The Coroner interpreted the verdict as one of manslaughter and committed the poor driver for trial on that charge. However, the magistrates found that there was not a *prima facie* case and he was discharged. At the Gloucester Assizes, the jury returned a formal verdict of 'not guilty'.

Sir John now had to reconsider his words a few years earlier about the desirability or otherwise of installing ATC. He recommended rather guardedly that ATC should eventually be adopted. His words deserved the serious consideration of the four main line companies, but did not lead to any action on their part (except for the Great Western). Pringle had been chairman of the Automatic Train Control Committee which had sat from 1920 to 1922, and he had also been Chairman of a second committee on the same subject, which commenced its work in 1927 and had still not completed its task by the time of the Charfield collision. By now, Col Sir John Pringle was an expert on Automatic Train Control, and his committee made a positive recommendation in favour of a fixed warning system of the Great Western type at distant signals, but very little came of it.

The conflicting evidence about the position of the arm of the Down distant signal illustrates clearly how difficult it is in such circumstances for the driver to prove his case. We shall never know the truth in the Charfield disaster. Did the driver really see a green light at the distant signal? Did he genuinely but mistakenly think that he had seen a green light? Or did he make up the story as an excuse? It is difficult to see how, in the circumstances, a green light could have been displayed. There may have been malicious interference but it seems highly unlikely, especially at that time in the morning. However, as part of their armoury of protective devices in the signalling system, the railway companies devised an additional safeguard, known as 'distant signal arm-proving'. The position of the distant signal arm was generally repeated in the signalbox by an electrical indicator, and this was subsequently used to provide a control on the block instruments in such a manner that a 'Line Clear' could not be given to the signalbox in rear unless the distant signal arm indicator was showing 'On'. It was a simple but effective additional safeguard and not expensive, and the Inspectorate should have pressed the railway companies to adopt it more quickly, if only to reassure drivers.

The Inspectorate's concern about fire was quite naturally intensified by the Charfield accident, and Sir John Pringle was sufficiently moved to remark that progress in phasing out the use of gas as an illuminant had not in all cases been so rapid as was desirable. It is interesting to speculate on what the outspoken Col Yolland would have had to say about it! The returns for November 1928 showed that the percentages of gas-lit carriages still in use were as follows:

LMS   50%
LNER 54%
GWR 67%
SR   30%

Many of these carriages were in use on branch lines, or were spare stock used on only a few occasions a year.

Less than three months later, whilst speculation on the Charfield disaster was still raging, there was another serious accident not many miles away on the same line, and by strange coincidence, with many of the same factors present. The train concerned was the sister train to the one involved at Charfield, being the 7.20pm Up express mail Bristol to Leeds, headed by LMS Standard Compound No 1060 and marshalled:-

Passenger coach
6-wheeled brake van

Passenger coach
Four 6-wheeled and bogie vans
Two passenger coaches
Three Post Office vans
Two Brake vans
Total: 14 vehicles, 313 tons.
There were 45 passengers in the train and a number of Post Office travelling staff.

Ashchurch lies on the Birmingham to Bristol line about seven miles north of Cheltenham, and in 1929 there were junctions to Evesham and Tewkesbury. There were two signalboxes — Ashchurch Junction, and Ashchurch Crossing 170 yards to the north. On 8 January 1929 the 6.25pm through freight Gloucester to Birmingham, headed by Midland Class 3F 0-6-0 No 3562, arrived at Ashchurch at 7.20pm and started to shunt at the Crossing signalbox. There was patchy fog, which was becoming worse, and the fogsignalmen were sent for at 8.25pm.

After the passage of the 'First Mail', the 8.5pm Gloucester to Birmingham, at about 8.40pm, it was decided to transfer some wagons from the Up sidings at Ashchurch Crossing signalbox to the Down sidings at Ashchurch Junction, and the engine drew 24 wagons out on to the Up Main line, preparatory to propelling them through the crossover on to the Down Main line.

Meanwhile, the signalman at Ashchurch Junction had accepted the Bristol Mail from Cleeve signalbox, as he was fully entitled to do even without his fogsignalmen on duty (they had not yet arrived at their posts), because he had received 'Train Out of Section' from the crossing signalbox for the previous train, and the block indicator was in the normal position. This was rather a trap, because the two signalboxes were only 170 yards apart, and the regulations were subsequently amended.

At 8.59pm the Mail passed Cleeve, at about 50mph, and the signalman sent the 'Train entering Section' signal to Ashchurch Junction. The shunting movement at the crossing signalbox was occupying the same line, and the signalman at the Junction thereupon left the signalbox with his handlamp and detonators to carry out Rule 85 (ie the placing of a detonator on the line during fog when the train cannot be allowed to proceed). Perhaps he had a niggling doubt in his mind; the shunting movement on the Up Main line was only 350yd beyond his Inner Home signal and the Mail was approaching in darkness and fog at full speed. He had gone less than 100yd down the line when he heard the Mail approaching. It was 9.10pm. Nonetheless, despite the weather conditions he had no reason to expect that the Mail would fail to stop at his home signal. Trains had always stopped before. Why should tonight be any different? But it was going to be. In fact it was going to be the worst night of his life. He just had time to put down a detonator when the train swept past him at 50 or 60mph.

At the Mail's last stop — Cheltenham — the fireman had looked back for the guard's signal, the engine being right-hand drive, and he now takes up our story. It was no more than hazy at Cheltenham, he said afterwards, and approaching Cleeve he saw a green light, which he assumed was the Cleeve Up

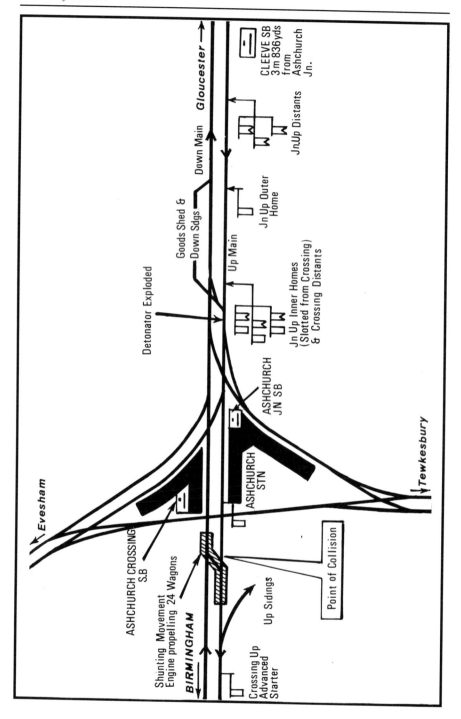

distant signal. He then did some firing and, on looking over the side, thought that the fog seemed to be getting thicker. He did a bit more firing then looked out again and realised that the fog was quite dense. A few seconds later he heard the explosion of a detonator and shouted to his mate 'Whoa'. Almost immediately he saw the lights of Ashchurch station and a few seconds later the Mail plunged into the wagons on the crossover.

The resulting wreck was quite exceptional and eight of the first nine coaches of the Mail were virtually destroyed. The engine fell over on to its side and the remains of the first eight coaches came to rest round it like the spokes of half a bicycle wheel. Fortunately there was no fire, but considering the wreckage it is little short of a miracle that only three of the train's 45 passengers were killed, although many people were injured, including members of the Post Office staff. The driver of the Mail was also killed.

It fell to Lt-Col Mount, now Chief Inspecting Officer following Sir John Pringle's retirement, to investigate this accident. He first had to satisfy himself that Ashchurch Junction's Up distant was at danger when the Mail approached and he came to the conclusion that it was. Considering the evidence it has to be said that it would have been difficult to have come to any other conclusion, and of course that was the key factor. He remarked 'This is another instance similar to that of Charfield, which confirms the utility of Automatic Train Control as affording, under modern conditions, desirable assistance to the driver, particularly when running in fog. A system like that which is installed at the distant signal on some sections of the GWR would assuredly have prevented this accident'. However, the railway companies turned a deaf ear and the Inspectorate did not press the point. The LMSR was putting its faith in colour-light distant signals, which were much easier to observe in fog, but that was only part of the answer. Accidents were to continue to occur, both in clear weather and in fog, even with colour-light distants, as we shall see in succeeding chapters. But fog was, and continued to be, the great enemy.

Statistical Summary 1915-1929

Year	Miles of line open	No of passengers killed in train accidents	No of railway staff killed Train accidents	Other causes	No of passengers carried exc season tickets (million)
1915	23,709	269	9	403	—
1916	—	3	12	402	—
1917	—	12	5	331	—
1918	—	8	5	293	—
1919	—	3	7	318	1,523
1920	23,734	6	5	371	1,579
1921	23,723	18	11	220	1,229
1922	20,298	5	4	203	1,195
1923	20,314	3	9	201	1,236
1924	20,329	24	8	220	1,236
1925	20,431	—	14	242	1,233
1926	20,396	13	2	159	1,069
1927	20,400	27	2	200	1,175
1928	20,388	48	15	201	1,196
1929	20,419	3	14	205	1,236

Notes:

1 Up to, and including, 1921 the figures include the whole of Ireland. From 1922 onwards the figures relate only to Great Britain. Certain figures were not compiled during the wartime period of government control of the railways.

2 In 1925 one passenger was killed on the Metropolitan Railway.

3 Average freight tonnage 1925-29 was 320 million.

A Too Brief Renaissance

The 1930s began with a new team of Inspecting Officers under the Chief, Lt-Col Alan Mount, and they were to serve right through the period covered by this chapter. Col A. C. Trench had entered the Inspectorate in 1927, and he was joined by Lt-Col E. Woodhouse in 1930. Maj G. R. S. Wilson came on the scene in 1935. These four officers were responsible for the Railway Inspectorate's policy and views on railway safety until nationalisation in 1948.

Lt-Col G. R. S. Wilson CBE
Chief Inspecting Officer: 1949-58

George Wilson (Bob) was commissioned in the Royal Engineers in 1914 at the age of 18 and saw service in field companies in France and Macedonia during World War 1, after which he did a course on the Longmoor Military Railway in Hampshire. After serving in the Transportation Branch of the War Office he was appointed an Assistant Inspecting Officer of Railways in 1935.

He returned to the army in 1939 as Assistant Director of Railways with the British Expeditionary Force in France until the evacuation from Dunkirk in June 1940, when he resumed his Inspection job, being appointed an Inspecting Officer in 1941.

Bob Wilson was something of a railway 'buff'. In this schooldays he contrived to frequent a certain Wiltshire signalbox, and he continued throughout his life to correspond with the signalman who first taught him the rudiments of railway operation. His remarkable bent for mechanical engineering found expression in his delighted study of locomotives, of which he was a connoisseur, and he was completely at home on the footplate. One story told about him concerns the engine of the 'Sud Express' behind which he and his family were travelling to the Basque country on holiday. It developed a fault and the train came to a stand, whereupon Bob Wilson went to the front of the train and helped the driver to locate and adjust the fault.

He held the inquiry into the double collision at Harrow in 1952, the second worst disaster in the history of Britain's railways (the 1915 crash at Quintinshill was the worst). The initial Harrow collision might have been

93

prevented by ATC, and Col Wilson gave an interesting historical review of the development of the equipment from 1912 when the GWR system was coming into use on that railway, up to the time of the Harrow accident in 1952. Col Wilson pointed out that 28% of all fatalities in train accidents during that period might have been prevented had ATC been installed.

He spent much time checking the working of the new form of ATC and in pressing the Railway Executive to speed up its tests. Finally, in 1956, he at last had the satisfaction of recommending the adoption of the new equipment for installation on all the major main lines in the country.

Lt-Col Wilson initiated the investigation into level crossing protection which led to the introduction of lifting barriers worked manually or automatically by the approaching train.

At the time of his death in 1958 he had nearly completed his investigations into the collision earlier that year at St Johns, Lewisham, the third worst railway disaster in Britain. There is little doubt that the strain and distress occasioned by this last investigation contributed to his untimely death.

Lt-Col Wilson was the archetypal Inspecting Officer, who was keen on, and devoted to, his job, and unsparing of his energies.

Their concerns were still the same – the eradication of dangerous errors by drivers and signalmen, and improvements in the fire and collision-resistant qualities of carriages. Whilst the Inspectorate was keen to reduce the number of accidents, it was equally anxious to cushion passengers against the effects of collisions and derailments.

The 1930s started very auspiciously. Only a single passenger was killed in 1930 in a train accident, and only a total of 17 lost their lives in the next three years. Whilst the causes were depressingly familiar, and whilst nearly all the fatal accidents could have been prevented by the application of existing technology, such a good safety record gave no grounds for a heavy programme of capital investment in safety measures, at a time when the railways were increasingly suffering from the effects of unbridled road competition and a world slump in trade.

However, it would be wrong to give the impression that the railways were doing nothing during the 1930s to increase safety. Quite the reverse, in fact. They were quietly installing track circuits and block signalling controls on a large scale, and replacing semaphore distant signals with colour-lights to ease the driver's heavy burden during darkness and fog. Such weather conditions had been, and continued to be, common contributory causes of accidents. In suburban areas, multiple-aspect colour-light signals were being introduced in large numbers. Whilst these various measures also helped the signalman by providing safeguards against errors on his part, it was thought that colour-light signals would be of great assistance to drivers. This was certainly the case during fog and darkness, but colour-light signals were not 100% effective by themselves, as we shall see, and they needed the reinforcement of ATC. Paradoxically, the Great Western put its faith in semaphore distants with ATC until virtually the end of its independent existence, and its splendid safety record speaks for itself. From 1923 to 1947, excluding the war years, there were only two fatal train accidents on the GWR, and only one passenger was killed in each, an unparalleled record.

The only fatal train accident in 1930 occurred on 6 March, on the Settle to Carlisle line between the wayside stations of Culgaith and Langwathby. Although the 2,930ft high Cross Fell broods over the site, this is the rich, fertile country of the Eden Valley.

An engineer's ballast train, consisting of Class 4F 0-6-0 No 4009, with 15 ballast wagons and two brakevans, had been working in the 164yd long Waste Bank Tunnel, and had been protected by a flagman who had put detonators on the line not far from Culgaith. When he realised that the train would have to be shunted out of the way for the 8.5am local passenger train from Hellifield to Carlisle he picked up the detonators and set off back to the ballast train. He should not have done so, and the detonators should have remained on the line until the flagman had been told that the ballast train had been shunted clear of the main line, but the difficulties in communicating messages to an isolated flagman can be imagined.

And so the first line of defence was removed, but there remained the very substantial second line of defence – the signalling system, which should have ensured that the local train could not leave Culgaith until the ballast train had been shunted clear at Langwathby, almost 3½ miles away.

At about 10.0am the local train ran into Culgaith station. It was headed by 'Claughton' class 4-6-0 No 5971 and consisted of five vehicles, with 25 passengers. After a few parcels had been dealt with the guard waved his green flag and the train set off. The signalman's heart suddenly sank into his boots. His starting signal was clearly still at danger and he watched in alarm and horror as the train set off and accelerated past it. The second line of defence had gone, but there was still a remote chance that the ballast train would reach the protection of Langwathby's signals before the Claughton bore down on it.

Running easily on the gently-falling gradients, the local entered the 661yd-long Culgaith Tunnel, and then emerged into the daylight for the quarter-mile open stretch before again plunging into the darkness of Waste Bank Tunnel, a darkness which concealed the black bulk of the stationary 0-6-0 at the Culgaith end of the ballast train. Without any warning, the Claughton rammed the 0-6-0 at 35mph. The 4-6-0's driver lost his life in the crash and one passenger was killed. Four were seriously injured. Fortunately, there was no fire, although three of the five vehicles of the local were gas-lit.

Col Trench held a public inquiry into this accident, but found it difficult to recommend any new measures that might be taken to prevent a recurrence. Accidents caused by drivers wrongly passing starting signals at danger have punctuated railway history almost to the present day. Co-acting detonators at the starting signal, automatically placed on the line when the signal was at danger, might well have prevented this type of accident, but the railways felt that its relative infrequency did not justify the expenditure of providing the equipment, except in isolated cases. This was yet another instance where the Inspectorate had to weigh in the balance the cost of providing equipment to prevent a small number of accidents, against an unknown number of lives that would be saved. The railway companies themselves faced the same difficult

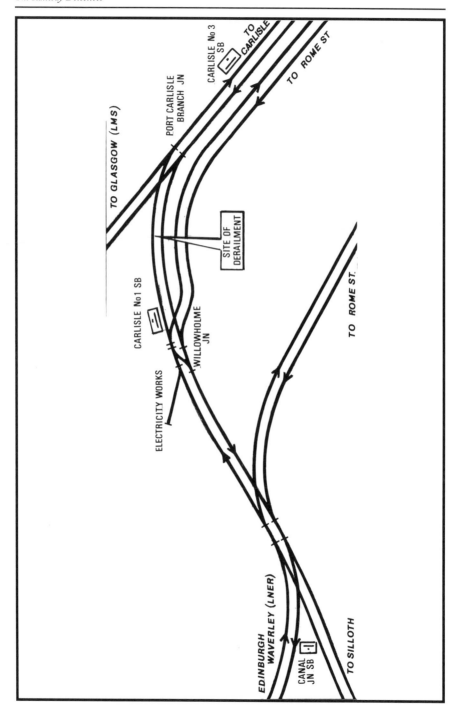

decision-area, but it was always easier (and still is) to do nothing until a particularly serious accident, or a series of accidents from the same cause, forced them to take action.

1931 was notable for two fatal derailments at high speed, reminiscent of the early years of the century. Lt-Col Mount investigated both. The first one took place on 3 January at Carlisle Canal when the 12.0 noon Edinburgh Waverley to St Pancras was derailed at 45-50mph on the sharp 15mph curve between Carlisle Nos 1 and 3 signalboxes. The train consisted of seven coaches, headed by 'Shire' class 4-4-0 No 2758 *Northumberland,* and the first four coaches were wrecked. Fortunately the train was lightly loaded, but three of the 35-40 passengers were killed. The Coroner's Inquest returned a verdict of manslaughter against the driver but he was acquitted at Carlisle Assizes.

Lt-Col Mount considered what could be done to help drivers in such circumstances. With considerable foresight he suggested that ATC warning apparatus fixed on the approach to permanent speed restrictions would ensure that drivers did not overlook them, but it was to take several more serious derailments before the railway authorities took such action over 40 years later. He also mentioned the advisability of keeping the distant signal at caution to ensure that drivers slowed down; a simple enough measure but one which could have led to an increase in signals passed at danger. In purist terms the purpose of the distant signal is to give the driver advance information about the home signal. If the distant signal is always at caution this valuable function is lost. Lt-Col Mount also recommended the erection of speed indicators or boards at the lineside, and the LNER subsequently adopted their well-known cut-out signs.

Whilst Lt-Col Mount was turning these ideas over in his mind there came news of the second derailment. This occurred at Leighton Buzzard on the LMSR West Coast main line at 12.20pm on Sunday 22 March 1931. The 11.30am express from Euston to Glasgow and Edinburgh was to be diverted from the Down Fast line to the Down Slow line owing to engineering work and the signalman had set the route accordingly, but he had not cleared his signals. The train approached at 55mph, ran past the home signal at Danger and became derailed on the sharply-curved crossover. There were 183 passengers on the train, together with 20 dining car and other railway staff. Three passengers and three railwaymen were killed in the resulting wreck.

In this accident there was no question of the driver's being misled or confused by the junction signals. It was a straightforward case of a signal being wrongly passed at danger and Lt-Col Mount said that it would have been prevented by ATC. The question of the signalling arrangements at facing junctions has always been a contentious issue, both in respect of regular timetabled movements, and those which are made without the driver's having been advised beforehand. It had long been the custom to provide directing distant signals so that the driver would know positively which way his train was being routed at a junction and giving him the opportunity to match the speed of this train to the speed required at the turnout. There were directing distant signals at Leighton Buzzard, but it subsequently became the practice to provide only one distant signal, which could not be cleared for the lower-speed route.

Another of those accidents with familiar overtones occurred on the LMS Midland Division near Crich Junction at 12.9am on 17 June 1933. Crich Junction lay 533yd north of Ambergate North Junction on the main line from Clay Cross to Derby, and controlled the Junction to Pye Bridge on the Erewash Valley line.

The 10.0pm express and mail from Leeds to Bristol (the same train as the one involved in the Charfield disaster in 1928) was that night composed of four brakevans, four passenger coaches and three Post Office vehicles, all electrically lit. It was double-headed by Class 2P 4-4-0 No 522 (pilot engine) and Standard Compound 4-4-0 No 1072.

The signalman at Wingfield, three miles north of Crich Junction, was unable to clear his signals for the Mail because there was a mineral train in the section ahead. As the Mail approached his signalbox he stood ready to lower the home signal and when the train was 150yd away he slowly did so, although he had already concluded that the train was going rather fast. He then realised that the train was not going to stop at all, so he waved a red light frantically at the two drivers, but neither responded and the train sped past the starting signal, which was still at danger. It caught up with the slow-moving mineral train between Crich Junction's distant and home signals at a closing speed of 30-40mph. The two engines were thrown on to their sides, killing both drivers, but because the Mail was lightly loaded there were no passenger deaths.

The gaps in the railway's safety defences had been cruelly exposed. There was no ATC at Wingfield distant signal to warn the driver. There were no detonator placers at Wingfield to help the signalman to warn the drivers. And of course there were no co-acting detonators at the starting signal. By contrast there were many safety devices in the signalbox, including

- 'Line Clear' release, which meant that the starting signal could not be lowered until Crich Junction had placed his block indicator to the 'Line Clear' position.
- The Wingfield signalman could not place his block indicator to 'Line Clear' unless his home signal lever was in the normal (danger) position.
- The signal levers were sequentially locked, so that they could only be cleared in the prescribed sequence, ie home, starter, distant.

Col Trench said that the accident would have been prevented by ATC, and he criticised the signalman for clearing his home signal before being sure that the Mail had been brought quite or nearly to a stand at it (Rule 40a) although it is doubtful in this case whether either of the drivers saw it. Most regrettable, though, was the absence of detonator-placers, and Col Trench was less severe in his criticism of the LMS than he ought to have been. Even as late as 1939 the LMS was saying that 'the desirability of equipping all signalboxes on the most important routes with this appliance is under review, although it had been decided to provide it in all new signalling schemes where conditions justify it'.

The LMS was in trouble again the following year when the signalman at Winwick Junction, on the West Coast main line just north of Warrington, forgot about a local passenger train standing at his Down home signal and wrongly

gave 'Train out of Section' for it. He then accepted the following train, the
5.20pm express Euston to Blackpool, which collided at full speed with the
slowly-moving local train, killing 10 passengers and a guard. A track circuit
would have prevented the accident, but Col Trench quite reasonably did not
criticise the LMS on this occasion. He commented that the company had made
very rapid progress with the provision of track circuits, but they naturally had
to place the proposals in order of urgency, and Trench considered the Winwick
Junction home signals to be low in the priority order. The signalbox was due to
be reconstructed in 1935, to full modern safety standards, including extensive
track-circuiting. Ironically, detonator-placers had been provided at Winwick
Junction, but they were of no use on this occasion.

A signalman's hasty error, similar to the one at Winwick Junction, caused a
major pile-up near King's Langley on the same main line on 13 March 1935,
involving no fewer than four freight trains:

1   The 4.55pm express meat train from Liverpool Alexandra Dock to Broad
    Street, 42 brake-fitted wagons, hauled by rebuilt 'Claughton' No 5946
    (bell-signalled 1-1-3).
2   The 5.50pm milk train Stafford to Euston, 22 tanks and vans, fully-fitted,
    hauled by Standard Compound 4-4-0 No 1165 (bell-signalled 1-1-3).
3   The 10.30pm fitted freight Camden to Holyhead, 45 vehicles (the first 14
    brake-fitted) hauled by 'Patriot' class '5XP' 4-6-0 No 5511 (bell-signalled 5
    consecutively).
4   The 12.25pm coal train Toton to Willesden, 70 wagons, hauled by Standard
    Class 7F 0-8-0 No 9598 (bell-signalled 4-1).

The signalling equipment on the line contained all the modern safeguards of
interlocking and block controls except, crucially, one. There was nothing to
prevent a signalman from concluding that a train had passed, when it had not
done so. No rotary block. No Sykes lock and block.

At about 11.0pm the meat train failed in the section on the Up Fast line
between Nash Mills and King's Langley signalboxes, owing to an engine defect.
The signalman at King's Langley became confused, jumped to the conclusion
that the train must have passed him, and gave 'Train out of Section' to Nash
Mills. The signalman there immediately offered the following milk train and
cleared all his signals for it. Two minutes later it passed Nash Mills signalbox,
and a minute after that it crashed headlong into the stationary meat train at
about 25mph, scattering its wagons far and wide. Almost immediately the
Holyhead freight, running on the Down Slow line at 40mph, ran into the
wreckage, whilst a few seconds later the coal train, travelling on the Up Slow
line at 25-30mph, added to the general pandemonium, in which three engines
were derailed and 75 wagons were piled up and destroyed or damaged. The
innocent driver of the milk train was killed.

The 10.50pm express from Euston to Edinburgh and Aberdeen was now due,
and might have turned what was almost a farce (apart from the death of a
driver and the cost to the LMS) into a nightmare, but luckily the King's
Langley signalman began to have doubts about his acceptance of the milk train

and he kept his signals at danger for the express on the Down Fast line. It was fortunate that he did so, as that line was well and truly blocked by wrecked and derailed wagons. Lt-Col Mount had no recommendations to make, other than the obvious one of saying that signalmen should do their jobs properly. However, he was given an opportunity to redeem himself a few months later, following his inquiry into a collision from a similar cause, a few miles across country at Welwyn Garden City on 15 June 1935.

The signalman there jumped to the conclusion that the 10.53pm King's Cross to Newcastle express had passed his signalbox whilst in reality it was still in the rear section and had not yet reached the track circuit at his outer home signal. He therefore wrongly gave the 'Train out of Section' signal to Hatfield No 3 signalbox and was immediately offered, and accepted, a following express, the 10.58 King's Cross to Leeds. The Newcastle train was slowly moving forward through the station and past the signalbox because the distant signal had been at caution, when it was run into in the rear by the Leeds express, at a closing speed of about 50mph. Some telescoping took place, as a result of which 12 passengers and two railwaymen lost their lives. The Welwyn Garden City signalman, having wrongly accepted the second express from Hatfield No 3 signalbox, had then cleared all his signals for it.

Welwyn Garden City station and signalbox had been built about 10 years previously and the signalbox was equipped with all the modern signalling safeguards, except, as at King's Langley, the critical one of proving that a train had actually passed through the section. It was to this that Lt-Col Mount now turned his attention. He recommended that the track circuit at the home signal should control the block instrument in such a way that a second 'Line Clear' could not be given until the first train had occupied and cleared this track circuit, thus proving that it had passed through the section. In effect the track circuit would perform the same function as the treadle in rotary and 'lock and block' systems. This was a major step forward and the system became known ever afterwards as 'Welwyn' control. It closed the loophole which had allowed the Winwick Junction, King's Langley and Welwyn accidents to happen and was the last in the battery of safeguards which had started to be applied to the signalling system almost a century earlier. From then on, the absolute block signalling system with all the safeguards applied was very safe indeed, but still required signalmen to be vigilant, as one of the Great Western's rare fatal accidents the following year was to demonstrate.

On 15 January 1936 the 10.30pm special mineral from Aberdare to Old Oak Common, with 53 wagons of coal headed by 2-8-0 No 2802, broke in two after passing Swindon. The rear portion of five wagons and the brakevan came to rest about half a mile before passing Shrivenham, but unaccountably neither the signalman at the box there, nor at Ashbury Crossing signalbox 1,122yd to the east, noticed the absence of tail and side lights. Each man therefore gave 'Train out of Section' for the mineral train and accepted the 9.0pm sleeper from Penzance to Paddington, which was following hard on the heels of the mineral train. All signals were cleared for the sleeper and disaster was inevitable unless the guard of the mineral train had gone back waving a red light. Unfortunately he hadn't. At 5.25am the sleeping car express, hauled by 4-6-0 No 6007 *King*

William III, crashed into the brakevan and wagons at about 55mph, killing the driver and a passenger. There was little that Lt-Col Mount could do, other than to criticise the two errant signalmen. Yet again he mentioned flares. If the mineral train guard had used one it might have been seen by the driver of the express in sufficient time for him to have stopped clear. Mount mentioned that there had been extensive tests of flares and Very lights on the GWR after the Dinwoodie crash in 1928, but after full consideration it was concluded that their provision was not justified, that they were of limited utility and had other disadvantages. The main problem would have been having them instantly to hand when needed. Lt-Col Mount also mentioned that the GWR had now installed ATC on 2,300 miles of main line. Incidentally, this was the last fatal peacetime accident on the GWR.

Col Trench was in action later the same year investigating a train fire. The 4.58pm Channel Islands boat train from Southampton Docks to Waterloo, with 350 passengers, had just passed through Winchester at about 45mph, when fire and smoke were observed by passengers in the second and third coaches. The communication cord was pulled and as the train came to a stand passengers jumped out to escape from the fire. As they did so a train came by on the other line and several passengers narrowly escaped being run down. The first four coaches were burnt down to their underframes. The cause was a relatively new hazard — an electrical defect.

1937 was one of those bad years that occasionally afflict the railways, 49 passengers being killed in four separate accidents. The worst one was at Castlecary on the ex-North British line of the LNER. At 4.37pm on 10 December the 4.3pm express from Edinburgh to Glasgow ran past Castlecary's home signal at danger at 65-70mph and crashed into the 2.0pm passenger train from Dundee to Glasgow, which was standing in rear of the starting signal. At that speed there was inevitably a great deal of wreckage, and of the 110 passengers in the Dundee train 22 were killed. Thirteen of the Edinburgh train's 198 passengers met the same fate, in the worst peacetime railway disaster ever up to that time on the British mainland (excluding the Tay Bridge collapse). There was some dispute about the position of the distant signal arm at Castlecary. It was not repeated in the signalbox (ie there was no indicator showing whether the signal was at caution or not), nor did it have a control on the block instrument which would have prevented the signalman from giving 'line clear' if the signal arm had been in any position other than horizontal (ie caution). Despite both drivers protesting that the signal had been at 'clear', the driver of the Edinburgh train was charged with culpable homicide in the Edinburgh High Court on 30 March the following year. The next day the Lord Advocate withdrew the charge and the jury was directed to return a verdict of Not Guilty. Lt-Col Mount reported that certain aspects of the evidence were unsatisfactory and he doubted whether all the facts would ever be fully established. He recommended the installation of a system of ATC and the appropriate signalling controls as a means of avoiding such accidents in the future. 'Distant arm-proving', as it became known, with a control on the block instrument, was already installed on 31% of the signals on the Edinburgh-Glasgow line, and on 67% on the Edinburgh-Berwick line.

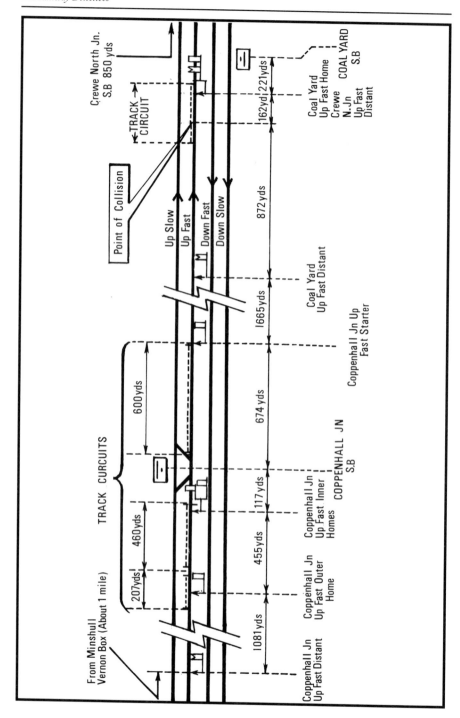

Fog, that eternal torment of the driver, was again present in an accident at Coppenhall Junction, just north of Crewe, during the night of 16-17 November 1937. It was particularly dense and trains were queuing up approaching Crewe from the north 'block and block'. The 2.30am from Liverpool was in the section between Crewe Coal Yard and North Junction signalboxes and the 10.30pm sleeping car express from Glasgow was standing at Coal Yard's home signal. The 8.30pm sleeping car express from Perth (which was later involved in two of Britain's worst rail tragedies, at Bourne End in 1945 and Harrow in 1952) was approaching Coppenhall Junction signalbox, about two miles to the north. Fogsignalmen were on duty at the distant signals, and the driver of the Perth train heard a detonator explode at Coppenhall Junction's distant, warning him that the signal was at caution. He saw one green light (which he took to be the home signal but was in fact the outer home) but did not see either the inner home or the starter, both of which were at danger. He saw the signalman waving at him, which he understood to mean that the starting signal was clear, but in fact the signalman had held both arms above his head, the handsignal for 'Stop', because the driver had run past the inner home signal at danger, a dangerous misunderstanding. The LMS had wisely installed detonator-placers at Coppenhall Junction, and the signalman had correctly operated one when he accepted the train. Both the signalman and a fogsignalman heard the detonator explode, but unfortunately the driver did not. He continued past the starter at danger into the section ahead and heard the fogsignalman's detonator explode at the Coal Yard distant. He was preparing to stop for the home signal when his fireman called out that there was a red tail lamp close ahead. He braked immediately but struck the rear of the Glasgow train almost at once. It was 4.25am. Fortunately there were no fatalities.

Maj G. R. S. Wilson held the public inquiry into the accident. The driver was clearly to blame for running past signals at danger, but there was some inevitable dismay that he had not heard the explosion of the signalman's detonator at Coppenhall Junction. The Inspectorate had been urging the railway companies for many years to install detonator-placers at signalboxes, yet now that the LMS had done so at Coppenhall Junction they were found to be ineffective. In fact the LMS had anticipated the problem and had started to provide two-shot detonator placers in new installations in order to increase the volume of sound. Maj Wilson recommended that existing equipment should also be modified.

These last few years before World War 2 were the streamlined era, and marked a period of welcome renaissance for the railway companies. They had overcome the upheavals of grouping; the years of depression were receding, and the companies were getting to grips with road competition. It is a matter of great regret that just when the railways were really getting their act together, war should have come along and put a stop to it all. It was a cruel act of fate and, as in 1914, things would never be the same again for the railways. Nevertheless, those war years were to see a rich flowering stemming from that renaissance. As had happened in World War 1, the railways' customary high safety standards were well maintained. The six years of war saw traffic levels 50% higher than pre-war and many experienced staff were called to serve in the

Left:
One of the enginemen of *King William III* GWR No 6007 looks back to see whether the signalman is going to clear his distant signal. The GWR persisted with semaphore distant signals but equipped them with automatic train control apparatus, in some ways a happy combination and preferable to a colour-light distant without ATC.

forces. Despite all the problems of bombing and the blackout only 140 passengers were killed in train accidents during the whole of the war, compared with 93 in the previous six years of peace and 220 in the first six postwar years. Lt-Col Sir Alan Mount had been knighted in 1941, and his comments in his Annual Report for 1944, written in July 1945, must have brought a glow of pride to all railwaymen. They are worth repeating:

'There can be no doubt that the services rendered by the railways contributed in no small measure to the success of the country's war effort. Besides normal transport activities connected with industry, vast movements of men and materials for the services were involved both before and during the build-up after the landing of the Allied Forces in France on 6th June. Compared with prewar, passenger miles increased by 68% and freight ton-miles by 47%. These unprecedented demands on the railways were met with depleted staffs and impaired equipment; their record is an eloquent tribute to their efficiency, standard of maintenance, and the high factor of safety attained, all of which reflect the greatest credit on every Railway man and woman for the part they played in this historic year.'

During the war years the work of the Inspectorate had naturally been on a reduced scale, with fewer public inquiries and inspections of major new works. After the war, it was time to look again at safety standards and to see where attention needed to be concentrated. Fog was still the railwayman's enemy, and whilst the spread of colour-light signalling was of some assistance, the lack of ATC on all railways except the GWR was a serious handicap, about which the three other companies seemed inclined to do little. Lt-Col Mount concluded his 1947 Annual Report by saying that there were substantial grounds for the extension of ATC and that it deserved high priority in relation to other operating and signalling improvements. He also mentioned that in October 1947 the GWR had demonstrated a modified form of ATC equipment designed to give three indications, green, double yellow and single yellow, so as to suit multiple-aspect colour-light signalling. The nationalised railway, formed in 1948, did not unfortunately develop the idea, the lack of differentiation between single and double yellow being a major factor in several accidents in later years.

The proportion of accidents attributable to signalmen was gradually declining, thanks to the continuing installation of such safety devices as track circuits, interlocked block ('Line Clear' release), Welwyn control, and other block control equipment.

Two accidents in 1944/45 indicated clearly that colour-light signals were not the complete answer to the perennial problem of drivers passing signals at danger, either in clear weather or in fog, and that only ATC could provide it. A wartime accident at Ilford, on the Liverpool Street to Ipswich line, on Sunday 16 January 1944, provided one of the first illustrations of the fallibility of colour-light signals during fog. The 2.40pm express from Norwich to Liverpool Street, composed of 12 coaches hauled by 'B12' 4-6-0 No 8564, ran past several colour-light and semaphore danger signals and collided at 20-25mph with the 2.38pm express from Yarmouth to Liverpool Street. Nine passengers were

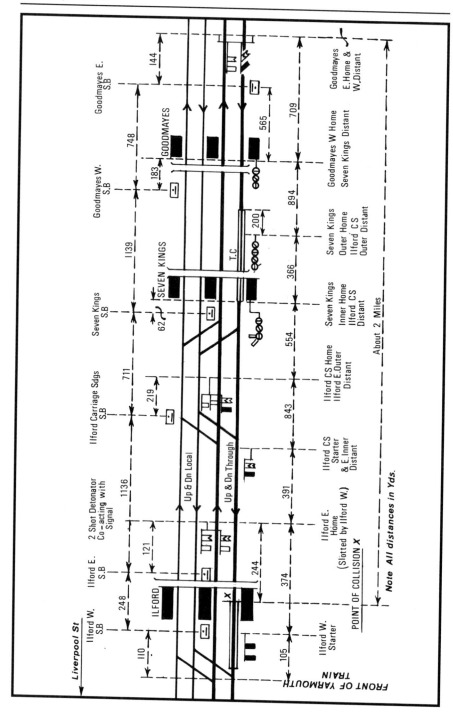

killed. There were no fogsignalmen on duty and double block-section working was in force, which is a method of keeping a clear section between two trains, as a partial safeguard against a driver's missing the signals at one signalbox. The line was equipped with Sykes 'lock and block' signalling equipment. Lt-Col Sir Alan Mount and Maj Wilson both had a hand in the Inquiry and could do no other but point out that ATC would have prevented the accident.

The following year there occurred what at the time was Britain's worst-ever peacetime rail disaster after Tay Bridge, and concerned a special use of double-yellow colour-light distants. As we have already seen in these pages, the method of signalling facing junctions had been in dispute for many years. Originally most junctions were provided with a separate distant arm for each route, and this gave a positive message to drivers. If no arm was lowered, the home signal was at danger. On the other hand if either arm was lowered the driver could then tell for which route the facing points were set, and if a speed reduction was necessary through a diverging junction the driver could brake accordingly. However, if for any reason the driver omitted to reduce speed there was a risk of derailment, and to overcome this danger some railway companies had decided to have only a single arm at the distant signal, to be cleared only for the straight route. This caused little or no delay where the driver had a good long view of the home signal, and where the points were immediately beyond the signal, but in other circumstances it could lead to some delay if the driver had to reduce speed prematurely, especially where an outer home signal was provided, and this could be an unacceptable situation on a busy four-track main line. Following an accident at Great Bridgeford in June 1932 the LMS had introduced a new signalling definition in connection with distant signals. At certain places they replaced semaphore splitting distants with a double-yellow colour-light distant, and drivers were told that the exhibition of two yellow lights meant:

'Pass the next signal at restricted speed, and if applicable to a junction may denote that the points are set for a diverging route . . .'

On Sunday 30 September 1945 the 8.20pm Perth to Euston sleeper approached Bourne End on the Up Fast line at about 65mph. The signalman had set his route from Up Fast to Up Slow, because engineers were working on the Up fast line in Watford Tunnel, and he had cleared his Up Fast outer home and his Up Fast to Up Slow inner home junction signal. His Up Fast distant showed two yellows. The train came on at full speed and started to go through the 20mph crossover at almost 60mph. It was too much to hope that the train could hold the rails at such a speed. The engine, 'Royal Scot' class 4-6-0 No 6157 *The Royal Artilleryman*, rolled over into a field, killing both enginemen. Six of the seven leading coaches piled up and were destroyed. Of the 398 passengers on board, 41 were killed and 64 were seriously injured.

Sir Alan Mount investigated this accident. His observations regarding the signalling are masterly and well repay the closest study for anyone wishing to go into the subject in more detail. He also had quite a lot to say about ATC and suggested that the accident would not have happened if there had been warning control at the distant signal. Inspecting Officers' reports on serious accidents are valuable not only for the logical and lucid manner in which they proceed to conclusions about the cause, but also for the observations on the history of the particular type of accident and the possible safeguards. The LMS abandoned the special use of two yellow lights in connection with junction working.

Sir Alan Mount also investigated an odd triple collision which occurred at Potters Bar on the LNER East Coast main line just after 10.0pm on Sunday 10 February 1946. At that time the Up Slow line from Hatfield terminated just north of the station and there were only two lines through the platforms. The 9.32pm local train from Hatfield to King's Cross was approaching Potters Bar on the Up Slow line, with the signals at danger, whilst on the main lines all signals were cleared for the 9.45pm express from King's Cross to Edinburgh and the 5.0pm express from Bradford to King's Cross. The signalman at Potters Bar saw the local train run past his Inner Home signal at danger at about 20mph and to prevent it from crashing into the buffer stops at the end of the Up Slow line he threw his Up Main line signals to danger and reversed the crossover to take the local train on to the Up Main line. He was just too late and moved the points under the first coach, which caused a derailment, fouling the Down Main line. Within a minute the Down express had crashed into the derailed coaches at about 45mph, then a minute later the Up express also ploughed into the wreckage. Fortunately its driver was on the alert and had seen the signals go back to danger, thus he was able to reduce his speed to about 10mph. Although there were 595 passengers in the Down express and 450 in the Up express, the only fatalities were two passengers in the lightly-loaded local train. Sir Alan Mount suggested that the LNER should press on with its plans for widening the line through Potters Bar so that there were four tracks instead of two. This was finally achieved eight years later in 1954.

1947, the last year of existence of the Big Four private railway companies, was one of the worst ever for passenger fatalities, in fact it was the worst peacetime year in the whole history of railways up to that point. On the Southern Railway 36 passengers were killed in four separate collisions (South Croydon, 24 October, 31 killed; Motspur Park, 6 November, 3 killed; Herne Hill, also 6 November, 1 killed; Farnborough, 26 November, 1 killed), which spoilt its very fine safety record — from 1923 to 1946 only 15 passengers had been killed in four collisions. The LNER fared no better, 52 passengers being killed in 1947 in three accidents. By contrast the Great Western ended its independent existence in triumph, with its fifth consecutive year free from fatal train accidents.

Errors by drivers and signalmen were among the causes but that demon, fog, was present on several occasions. Viewed from a 1990 standpoint, with colour-light signals, diesel and electric traction, and AWS, one can only marvel that drivers managed to run their trains at all during fog in years gone by, with oil-lit semaphore signals, steam locomotives and no ATC, yet run them they did, and with only very occasional lapses. One such lapse took place at Gidea Park, on the Liverpool Street to Colchester line of the LNER, at 11.17pm on 2 January 1947. There was dense fog, and some, but not all, fogsignalmen's posts were manned. As the 10.28pm train from Liverpool Street to Southend was starting from the station, a following train, the 10.25pm from Liverpool Street to Peterborough, ran into it at more than 30mph, wrecking the rear three coaches. Seven passengers were killed. The driver of the Peterborough train had run past the inner home and starting signals at danger at the previous signalbox, Romford, and had run past the outer home signal at Gidea Park, also at danger. In fact, he had not seen them at all in the fog. Lt-Col Woodhouse investigated this accident. Clearly the driver had been at fault, but the installation of ATC would have prevented the accident. He also said that it might also have been prevented by a much cheaper and simpler piece of equipment — a detonator-placer in Romford signalbox. Rule 94 stated:

'When the signalman requires to stop an approaching train during fog he must use his detonator-placer to put a detonator on the line.'

There were no detonator-placers at Romford, despite it being on a busy four-track main line, and despite the fact that the Inspectorate had been calling for the provision of such equipment since before World War 1. It was beginning to look as though a new 1889 Regulation of Railways Act was required, to force the railways to adopt ATC and to provide detonator-placers.

The Southern Railway's worst accident occurred on 24 October 1947 near South Croydon Junction on the main line from Brighton to London Victoria. Again, there was dense fog. The 7.33am electric passenger train from Haywards Heath to London Bridge had been standing for several minutes in Purley Oaks station at the starting signal, waiting acceptance by the South Croydon Junction signalman, and during this period passengers joined the train in quite large numbers. The existence of the train was overlooked by the signalman at Purley Oaks, and when he was asked by the signalman at the next box, Purley North, 'How he was looking on the Up Main', he thought that he had forgotten to give 'Train out of Section', which he promptly did, and accepted the following electric train, the 8.4am Tattenham Corner to London Bridge. At this moment the South Croydon Junction signalman accepted the Haywards Heath train (which the Purley Oaks signalman thought referred to the Tattenham Corner train), whereupon the signalman at Purley Oaks cleared all his signals.

The driver of the Haywards Heath train, still standing in Purley Oaks station, saw the starting signal cleared, assumed naturally enough that it had been cleared for him, and set off. By this time the Tattenham Corner train was hard on his heels and caught up with him 366 yards short of South Croydon Junction signalbox. The Haywards Heath train consisted of eight coaches and was carrying about 800 passengers (seats for 536). The Tattenham Corner train had nine coaches, 1,000 passengers and 750 seats. The collision took place at a closing speed of about 25mph, resulting in the rear coach of the first train and the leading coach of the second being wrecked. The deaths included 31 passengers and the driver of the second train.

Sir Alan Mount had the task of unravelling the mystery. The line was equipped with Sykes 'lock and block' equipment, which should have made it impossible for the signalman at Purley Oaks to have accepted a second train whilst he still had one standing at his starting signal. However, there was a

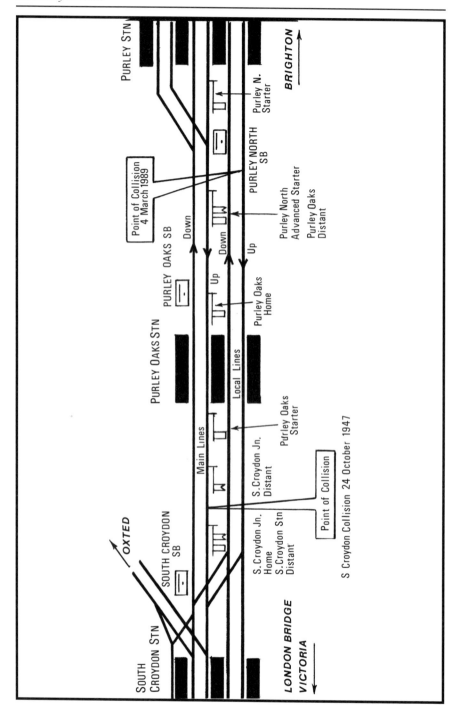

safety loophole in the system, which we have seen before. In order to be able to restore the equipment to normal after a train which had been accepted was subsequently cancelled, or to overcome the effect of locking during an equipment failure, a release key was provided for the signalman to use and free himself. Unfortunately it was too fatally easy to rush to the release key without sufficient thought, and that is what the signalman had done on this occasion. The Southern Railway had taken the situation so seriously that they had issued an instruction the previous year that improper use of the release key would render the signalman liable to dismissal.

However, it had not been a deliberately considered act on the signalman's part, but rather an impetuous action whilst confused. Purley Oaks was the signalman's first signalling post and he had been there for only five months. Significantly he had not had any experience of working a signalbox in fog. The situation of having to put inexperienced men into main line signalboxes was a product of the postwar labour market.

Sir Alan Mount added that but for the war, colour-light signalling and track circuiting would have been installed between Battersea Park and Coulsdon in 1940 (it was eventually done in 1955). He also said that no mechanical system other than Sykes' could have coped so efficiently with such heavy train services. His report also gives a detailed description of the method of operation of the Sykes' system.

Two days later, on Sunday 26 October, another exceptionally serious accident was added to the melancholy catalogue of disaster, at Goswick on the East Coast main line, about six miles south of Berwick. The signalman had set his points from the Up Main to the Up Independent line because of engineering work ahead. The driver of the 11.15am express from Edinburgh to King's Cross failed to see the distant signal at caution and took the points at much too high a speed, as a result of which a general derailment took place, with the engine, 'A3' class Pacific No 66 *Merry Hampton*, and eight coaches plunging down a low bank into a ditch. There were 15 coaches and 420 passengers on the train, of which 27 passengers and a train attendant lost their lives. Sir Alan Mount was fully occupied with the South Croydon Inquiry, therefore Col Trench and Lt-Col Wilson held the inquiry into the Goswick accident, which was added to the long list of accidents that would have been prevented by ATC.

There were two more fatal accidents a few days later on 6 November, on the Southern Railway. This spate of four fatal accidents in two weeks would have created an almighty furore had it happened in 1990, with calls for the resignation of the Secretary of State for Transport and demands that a formal public inquiry be set up, but all this happened before the days of mass television, and the public, having recently survived far worse horrors, took things in its stride, as did the Inspectorate. And so, on 31 December 1947 the 'Big Four' passed into history, with many a nostalgic backwards glance. No doubt, as they switched off the lights in their offices on that New Year's Eve the quartet of long-serving Inspecting Officers, Lt-Col Sir Alan Mount, Col Trench, Lt-Col Woodhouse and Lt-Col Wilson looked back to some of the more outstanding accidents and inquiries of the previous quarter of a century, and wondered what changes were to come under the British Railways regime. They need not have worried. For several years it was going to be a case of *Plus ça change, plus c'est la meme chose.*

Statistical Summary 1930-1947

Year	No of passengers killed in train accidents	No of railway staff killed Train accidents	Other causes	No of Passenger trains Collisions	Derailments
1930	1	4	204	79	56
1931	8	13	146	64	79
1932	4	3	167	63	70
1933	5	11	152	85	58
1934	17	12	204	81	51
1935	13	7	165	75	47
1936	3	17	195	104	62
1937	49	11	178	107	68
1938	11	7	193	68	51
1939	9	8	209		
1940	40	8	240		
1941	50	7	264	Figures not	
1942	27	9	242	available during	
1943	4	5	251	the war	
1944	12	8	255		
1945	45	17	221		
1946	34	9	227	90	70
1947	93	8	210	103	82

Summary 1923-47

	No of fatal train accidents	No of passengers killed
LMSR	29	205
LNER	27	225
GWR	5	34
SR	11	70
Unallocated	—	9

Great Changes — New Problems

Nationalisation on 1 January 1948 brought comprehensive changes to the political and financial control and organisation of Britain's railways. As they now came under public ownership, and as the making of profits was no longer the ultimate aim (or so it was rather naïvely thought at first), more attention and more money could perhaps be devoted to safety. The newly-formed Railway Executive might have been expected to behave in such a responsible manner that the existence of an independent watchdog on safety such as the Railway Inspectorate could be considered superfluous. And indeed, the new men at Railway HQ quickly threw aside a half-century or so of vacillation and announced almost at once that they would embark on a programme to extend ATC (now called Warning Control) on main line routes. However, it very quickly became clear that finance for safety was not unlimited, when the Executive tempered their statement with an ominous remark that 'it should be initiated as *soon as circumstances would allow*'. Any lingering doubts that the Railway Inspectorate had become redundant were thus quickly dispelled. The new railway authority was faced with the same difficult decisions about investment in safety measures that had plagued previous railway managers, and a separate independent body, able to make judgements free from political, financial, and indeed any other pressures, was essential if the safety of the travelling public was to be properly taken into account. The duties and responsibilities of the Inspectorate were therefore unchanged and even its *modus operandi* was largely the same. Its routine and regular contacts were with the new Regional headquarters as successors to the main line companies, rather than with the Railway Executive, which was mainly consulted on national standards and issues, a situation which has continued until the present day.

For at least the next 10 years the main safety problems confronting the railways were the very familiar ones of collisions caused by drivers' and signalmen's errors. Then, as the appliction of modern signalling controls and ATC began to take efect, new perils arose from the introduction of new technologies, a process which became particularly marked in the 1960s.

An example of one of the familiar accidents in a familiar location took place at Winsford, on the West Coast main line about eight miles north of Crewe,

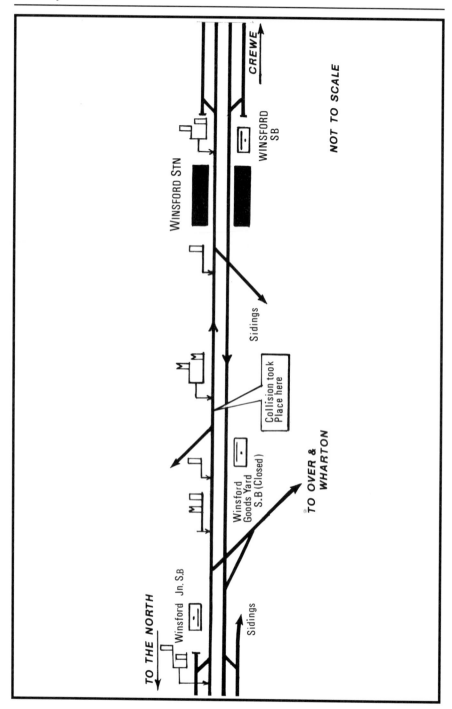

NOT TO SCALE

CREWE

WINSFORD STN

WINSFORD SB

Sidings

Collision took Place here

Winsford Goods Yard S.B (Closed)

TO OVER & WHARTON

Winsford Jn. S.B

TO THE NORTH

Sidings

shortly after midnight on 17 April 1948. The 5.40pm express Glasgow to Euston was halted in mid-section between Winsford Junction and Winsford Station signalboxes when a soldier who wanted to get home quickly (he lived nearby) pulled the communication cord. The signalman at Winsford Station signalbox then made a fatal error. Although he had not seen the train go past he assumed that it must have done so, and he sent 'Train out of Section' to Winsford Junction signalbox. It is a scenario that we have come across many times before in these pages. The Junction signalman immediately offered forward a following express, the 6.25pm Postal, Glasgow to Euston, of 13 bogie vans drawn by Pacific No 6251 *City of Nottingham*, and, upon having it accepted, cleared all his signals. The Postal entered the obstructed section at full speed but then the driver saw a red light ahead. It was the guard of the first train carrying out protection, but he had only covered about 400yd. The driver made an emergency brake application and had managed to reduce speed to 40-45mph when the collision occurred. The impact severely damaged the last two coaches of the standing train, killing or fatally injuring 24 of their occupants. Matters might have become worse still, as the Down Postal was closely approaching, but before the accident happened the Winsford Station signalman began to have doubts about his actions and he put his Down main line signals to Danger, thus bringing the Down Postal safely to a stand.

Lt-Col Wilson, who investigated the accident, had no particular recommendations to make, although 'Welwyn Control' would have prevented the accident. He did, however, raise yet again the question of the provision of flares, to be used by the guard in just such an emergency to warn an approaching driver of an obstruction ahead. He records in his report that the idea was still under consideration by the railway authorities.

Another type of accident which was to become increasingly familiar for the next 30 years until BR took action to prevent it, occurred on 18 November 1948 at Woolwich Arsenal on the Southern Region. The driver of the 12.28 electric multiple-unit (EMU) train started from Woolwich Dockyard station on receipt of the guard's 'Right away' hand signal, ran past the platform starting signal at danger into the section ahead, and collided with the 12.17 Cannon Street-Gravesend EMU, at not less than 15mph. Two people were killed. Col Trench attributed the accident to a lack of concentration on the driver's part, which led him to react to the guard's handsignal and fail to observe the platform starting signal. This type of accident became known as 'Ding-ding and away', taking its name from the two rings given by the guard on the bell communication to the driver. A similar accident occurred at Newcastle Central on 17 August 1951, when three people were killed. Lt-Col Wilson remarked in his report that there had been seven collisions of this nature in the last three years, but a solution to the problem eluded both BR and the Inspectorate.

1949 was a landmark for the Inspectorate. The Chief Inspecting Officer, Lt-Col Sir Alan Mount, retired on 31 July, after 30 years' service, including 20 years as Chief, the longest tenure in that post in the history of the Inspectorate, but he did not divorce himself entirely from railway safety, as he became a consultant to the Railway Executive on matters concerned with safety measures. However, that was not to last for long. He had continually overworked himself since the outbreak of war, and his health broke down to such an extent that he was practically an invalid until he died in 1955. Like so many Inspecting Officers, he was utterly devoted to his job and he worked himself relentlessly hard. Col Trench said of him afterwards that he had great charm of manner and took pride in the fact that ever since a Government Railway Inspectorate had been set up over 100 years ago its technical staff had been provided by officers of the Corps of Royal Engineers, pointing out that an adequate degree of Government supervision was exercised with the minimum of statutory powers and with an economy of staff unequalled in any other country. Col Trench, who himself retired in 1949, went on to say that it was in the daily routine of approval and inspection of new works, and discussion of safety measures, that Sir Alan Mount showed his talent for persuasion, and, most important, for maintaining and improving friendly co-operation with the railway companies' staff in the pursuit of the common aim of safety. He was justifiably proud of the outstanding record of the British railway companies in this respect, and of the share of the Inspecting Officers in contributing thereto.

Lt-Col Woodhouse also retired the same year, leaving Lt-Col Wilson, who now became the Chief, as the only link with the prewar railway. His colleagues were Brig C. A. Langley (1946-1963) and Col D. McMullen (1948-1968), both of whom became the Chief in their turn. They were later joined by Col W. P. Reed (1953-1968).

Brig C. A. Langley CB, CBE, MC
Chief Inspecting Officer: 1958-63

Charles Langley was born in Cork in 1897, the son of the Under-Secretary of State to the Egyptian Government. He was commissioned into the Royal Engineers in 1915, and served in France, being awarded the Military Cross twice.

He spent most of the inter-war years at the Longmoor Military Railway, becoming Chief Instructor, apart from a six-year spell, 1927-33, when he worked on the electrification of the Bombay-Poona line. During the war he held important posts in transportation in the Middle East, in India, and in South East Asia, for which he received the CBE (Commander of the British Empire).

In 1946 he retired from the army and became an Inspecting Officer, being promoted to Chief Inspecting Officer in 1958. Although he retired from the Inspectorate in 1963 he continued to be actively involved in rail transport affairs until he was in his 80s. He died in 1987.

Col D. McMullen
Chief Inspecting Officer: 1963-68

Dennis McMullen joined the Inspectorate in 1948. He succeeded Brig Langley as Chief Inspecting Officer in 1963, and retired in 1968. Some of the greatest changes on the railways, and challenges for the Inspectorate occurred during his five year tenure as CIO. Steam locomotives were replaced by diesels. The West Coast route became Britain's first main line to be electrified at 25kV ac; and there was large-scale modernisation of signalling. Under McMullen, the Inspectorate had to deal with the freight train derailment problem of the 1960s.

Accidents caused by the faulty maintenance of locomotives gave the Inspectorate great concern in the postwar years, one of the most serious being at Weedon, on the West Coast main line, on 21 September 1951. Pacific No 46207 *Princess Arthur of Connaught*, hauling the 8.20am express Liverpool to Euston, left the rails at 60-65mph owing to a bogie defect, resulting in the deaths of 14 passengers and a dining car attendant. The following year a tender brake rod came adrift and caused the derailment of the 9.15am 'Thames-Clyde Express' Glasgow to St Pancras at Blea Moor on 18 April 1952. The 10-coach train was double-headed by Compound 4-4-0 No 1040 and 'Royal Scot' class 4-6-0 No 6117 *Welsh Guardsman*. The Compound's loose brake rod struck and damaged the facing point lock stretcher bar, causing one of the switch blades to be opened sufficiently to cause derailment of the train, which was running at 65mph. Fortunately there was no loss of life, but there were many injuries.

The Western Region's fine record of freedom from fatal train accidents at last came to an end after 13 years on Sunday 20 November 1955, but only because a 'foreign' (ie BR Standard) engine was involved, 'Britannia' class 4-6-2 No 70026 *Polar Star*. The engine was hauling an excursion train from Treherbert to Paddington and was being diverted from the Up Main line to the Up Goods loop at Milton, near Didcot, because of engineering works. The engine took the turnout at excessive speed and became derailed, resulting in the deaths of 11 passengers. The driver was at fault and had failed to react to the ATC warning at the distant signal; and the automatic brake application had been overridden either by the driver himself or by the fireman. 'Britannia' class Pacifics differed from GWR locomotives in several respects and the driver was not really familiar with the changes.

A few days later, on 2 December 1955, there was another serious accident, this time at Barnes, on the Southern Region, which has some familiar features. Eleven passengers and two traincrew were killed when the 11.12pm EMU Waterloo to Windsor and Chertsey was irregularly admitted to the section between Barnes East and Barnes Junction signalboxes and ran into the 10.55pm freight train from Battersea to Brent, which was slowly moving forward. The line was equipped with Sykes' lock and block apparatus, and, as had happened on a number of previous occasions, the signalman had momentarily forgotten about the freight train and had used his release key to reset his block instrument to allow the signalman at the box in rear to clear his signals for the passenger train. The ability to reset without sufficient thought was the Achilles heel of the Sykes system. Neither the Midland rotary block system nor the Welwyn control system suffered from this defect. To release rotary block from the 'Train on Line' (or 'Train in Section') position requires the signalman to press a button which is recessed behind a piece of glass. To operate the button, the signalman has to break the glass, which is not undertaken lightly because it entails sending for a technician to replace the

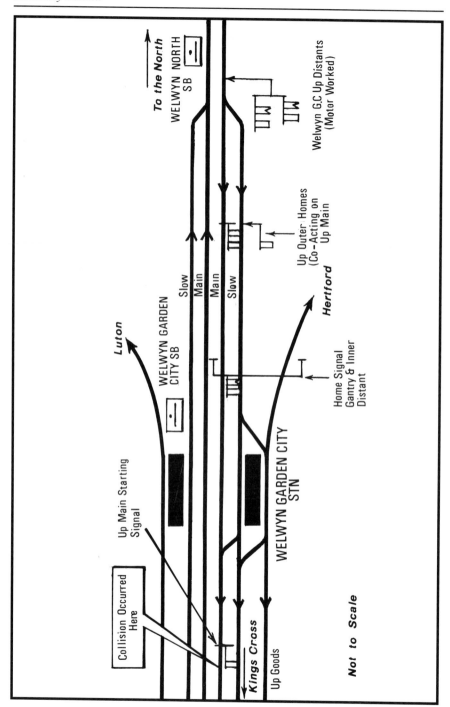

glass; and a report giving the reason for using the release has to be sent to the stationmaster. To release the block indicator under the Welwyn control system requires an indicator to be turned through 360°. The turning movement is generated by a small handle, which itself has to be turned about a hundred times, a laborious process giving plenty of time for reflection.

It will be recalled that the Welwyn control system was devised following a serious accident at Welwyn Garden City in 1935. There was another accident near that station on Monday 7 January 1957. The 6.18am six-coach local from Baldock to King's Cross, headed by 2-6-4T No 67741, had left the Up Slow platform and was then turned out on to the Up Main line as booked. The 7.10pm Aberdeen to King's Cross express was already closely approaching, having been accepted by the signalman up to his outer home signal, which was at danger; but it failed to stop there and continued past both that signal and the inner home. The signalman operated his emergency detonator-placer and heard the explosion, whilst the signalbox lad rushed to the window and held out a red lamp. Both were ignored by the driver and the train roared through the station at 65mph. It quickly caught up with the local train, which had accelerated to 30-35mph, and smashed into it, wrecking the last coach and killing one of the passengers. The express engine, Class A2/3 Pacific No 60520 *Owen Tudor*, turned over on to its side.

Lt-Col Wilson investigated this accident, and was faced by a claim by the express driver that the Up Distant was at 'clear', although he admitted that he missed the outer home and said that the inner home was blotted out by smoke and steam. The distant signal was a power-worked semaphore, located below the Welwyn North signals, and the arm had to be proved to be horizontal before 'Line Clear' could be given. After a very thorough investigation Lt-Col Wilson reached the conclusion that the signal had been at caution when the driver passed it.

There was some disappointment that the express driver had failed to react to the explosion of the twin detonators and it was recommended that larger detonators should be used. ATC equipment had already been installed at the distant signal but No 60520 had not yet been equipped. There was great faith that ATC would eventually eliminate such accidents, but there had been another warning only a few months previously that ATC was not 100% infallible.

On 6 September 1956, at Ludlow, the driver of the 2.0pm parcels train Penzance to Crewe, headed by an ex-GWR 2-6-0 No 9306, failed to react positively to an adverse distant signal, cancelled the automatic brake application, and continued forward at speed. He then passed two signals at danger and crashed into the 4.45pm express Penzance to Manchester at about 45mph. The express was stationary at the time. Fortunately there were no fatalities. There was some suggestion that the warning siren on the engine had become muffled by cotton waste, but this did not affect the automatic brake application, which must have been cancelled subconsciously by the driver. This accident, and the one at Milton a year earlier, were warnings that ATC was not completely foolproof, but there is no doubt that its benefits far outweighed any shortcomings. This was emphasised by two of the worst collisions in railway history, at Harrow & Wealdstone in 1952 when 108 passengers and four staff were killed, and at Lewisham St Johns in 1957, when 89 passengers and a guard were killed. Both these accidents have been fully described elsewhere; suffice it to say here that they would both almost certainly have been prevented if ATC had been in use.

However, as the installation of ATC proceeded (now known as the Automatic Warning System — AWS) coupled with the extension of multiple-aspect colour-light signalling, there was a corresponding reduction in the number of serious accidents caused by drivers' and signalmen's errors. But new concerns arose, particularly in the 1960s, such as buckled track, broken rails and freight train derailments. It would, perhaps be wrong to describe these as new perils, but they were intensified by the application of new technologies, such as continuously welded rails (CWR) and diesel locomotives. The automation of level crossings was also to be a matter which occupied a great deal of the Inspectorate's time and thoughts.

The method of operation of public level crossings had changed little in the previous 100 years, and the railway was still protected by massive gates which had to be swung across by signalmen or crossing keepers. The legal requirement to maintain attendance at public level crossings, imposed by the Railways Clauses Consolidation Act 1845, was not only a heavy financial burden on BR but caused other problems. In the postwar labour market it was often difficult to recruit and retain staff for the responsible but poorly paid and often boring job of crossing keeper, and the staff recruited were not always of the right calibre. The signalling and safety arrangements at many crossings were quite primitive, and whilst they were perhaps adequate for the horse and cart era their shortcomings were increasingly exposed as the volume of road traffic continued to grow. Furthermore, the need at many crossings to close the gates across the road several minutes before a train was due in order to give time for the signalman to clear his distant signal before it came within the engine driver's sight led to heavy delays to road traffic. There was therefore an urgent need to take action to improve the situation on three counts: to improve safety; to reduce or eliminate manning costs; and to reduce delays to road traffic.

In order to make progress the CIO asked Cols McMullen and Reed to visit Continental railways, accompanied by officers of BR and the Ministry of Transport, to study automatic level crossing installations and make recommendations. The visit took place from 4 to 13 October 1956 and the main recommendation which emerged was for a form of automation that became known as the automatic half-barrier installation, with the barriers being lowered automatically by the approach of a train. An Act of Parliament was therefore passed in 1957 allowing the introduction of such level crossing equipment without attendants, but development work was undertaken very cautiously and there was often considerable public opposition to what became known, somewhat disparagingly, as 'Continental level crossings'. The Inspectorate recognised that the education of the public, and the changing of public opinion, would be major and time-consuming tasks, and so they have turned out to be. The first automatic half-barrier (AHB) level crossing was brought into use at Spath, near Uttoxeter on 5 February 1961, and during the

1960s they were introduced in increasing numbers, so that by the end of 1967 some 200 had been installed, and there were plans to accelerate the programme. Then came a cruel blow.

On 6 January 1968, a massive road transporter lorry carrying a 120-ton transformer was proceeding very cautiously over an AHB crossing at Hixon, Staffordshire, when the red lights started to flash and the barriers to descend. The lorry was moving so slowly that it was unable to get clear before the train, a Manchester to Euston express, which had caused the barriers to lower, arrived at the level crossing, still travelling at almost full speed. The electric locomotive struck the transformer and hurled it aside, becoming derailed itself in the process. Several coaches were also derailed and 11 passengers were killed. BR should have been informed beforehand of the movement of the transporter lorry over the level crossing so that they could have taken special precautions, but no such prior notice was received.

The British public had always been suspicious of AHB level crossings and loved the old-fashioned gates. The Hixon accident, even though it was a million to one chance, confirmed their prejudices, despite widespread evidence from the rest of Europe of the safety of AHB crossings, and from Britain of the dangers of manned, gated crossings. By this time German Federal Railways had over 800 AHBs and the French Railways over 2,000. Nevertheless, the bizarre nature of the accident attracted tremendous public attention and the Government decided that a more formal inquiry should be held under the provisions of Section 7 of the 1871 Regulation of Railways Act. They appointed Mr E. B. Gibbens, QC to hold the inquiry, rather than one of the Inspecting Officers, because it was felt that as the Inspectorate had been so closely involved in formulating proposals for AHBs they could hardly be considered independent. In the circumstances it has to be considered a correct decision, even though it was the first time it had been done since the Tay Bridge disaster of 1879. The outcome was a confirmation of the policy of automating level crossings, but with additional, and in some cases unnecessary and irrelevant, safeguards which had the effect of defeating the policy of automation because the extra costs made it uneconomic for BR to do so. The automation programme came to a sudden stop and there was to be little or no progress for the next 10 years or so, during which time thousands of level crossings were automated on the West European railways.

Lt-Col Wilson died very suddenly on 20 March 1958 at the age of only 61, and, as in the case of Sir Alan Mount, the demands of the job took their toll. Lt-Col Wilson had to undertake the inquiries into two of Britain's worst rail disasters, both of which occurred in the 1950s — at Harrow in 1952 and at Lewisham in 1957. Few people realised the great strain that the Harrow disaster imposed upon him or appreciated the depth of his sympathy with all who suffered in that tragedy. His health was impaired by this profound investigation, but he resumed work after some weeks' rest. He did not live to complete his investigation into the Lewisham accident. Lt-Col Wilson was succeeded by Brig C. A. Langley, who completed the Lewisham Inquiry and retired in his turn in 1963 at the age of 65. He then began a third career as a transport consultant, being involved in the electrification of the Pakistan

Western Railways. As Managing Director of the UK Railway Advisory Service, a consultancy service set up by the Ministry of Transport, he travelled all over the world. He finally died at the age of 90, in 1987.

Col J. R. H. Robertson CBE
Chief Inspecting Officer: 1969-73

John Robertson was commissioned into the Royal Engineers in 1932 at the age of 20 and spent his prewar years at the Railway Training Centre, Longmoor. Wartime duties took him to France, Norway, India and South East Asia. His army career continued until 1958, when Lt-Col Wilson's untimely death gave him the unexpected opportunity of becoming an Inspecting Officer of Railways.

He suffered increasingly from arthritis and retired in 1973, having been Chief Inspecting Officer for five years, and died in 1977. He is remembered by many for the courageous way he overcame his physical disability, insisting on playing a full part in sometimes onerous inspections and accident investigations. This is epitomised by his inspections of the West Coast main line electrification, during which, in the depths of winter, he had himself strapped into a chair bolted to the flat roof of a wiring train so that he could view the clearances at bridges.

Lt-Col I. K. A. McNaughton BScEng, CEng, FIMechE, FCIT, FIRSE
Chief Inspecting Officer: 1973-82

Born in 1920, Ian McNaughton was commissioned as a Second Lieutenant in the Royal Engineers and his war service took him to Northwest Europe, for which he was mentioned in despatches. His military career also took him to the Middle East in 1949 (General Headquarters, Middle East Land Forces), and to Cyprus in 1955, after which he returned to Germany in 1960 to join the British Army of the Rhine.

He retired from the army and joined the Railway Inspectorate in 1962, becoming Chief Inspecting Officer in 1973, a post he held for nine years. During those nine years he saw a steady improvement in safety on BR, thanks to the extension of the automatic warning system and the continuing modernisation of signalling, among other things.

In 1977, recognising that the automation of level crossing protection had almost come to a full stop, he arranged for a joint Department of Transport/British Rail Working Party, headed by Lt-Col A. G. Townsend-Rose and Fred Walmsley (BR), to visit certain European railways to study their practices. The Working Party's report led to many changes, and allowed the progress of automation to be resumed.

Lt-Col Wilson and Brig Langley were succeeded by Col J. R. H. Robertson (1958-73) and Lt-Col I. K. A. McNaughton (1962-82). The Inspectorate was increased to five to cope with the increased workload: Maj P. M. Olver arrived in 1965, and he remained in the Inspectorate until 1989, having the distinction of being the longest-serving Inspector since Lt-Col Sir Alan Mount, who had retired 40 years earlier. The workload of the Inspectorate became much heavier during the 1960s owing to the large number of inspections of new works that were required, such as level crossing modernisation, station rebuilding, track remodelling, electrification and signalling modernisation, much of which arose from the BR Modernisation Plan of the mid-1950s. Furthermore, the railway system was becoming much more technically complex and the Inspectorate had to keep abreast of such developments.

The 1960s are remembered as the era of the freight train derailment problem, or to put it more precisely the derailment of short wheelbase four-wheeled freight vehicles running at speed on plain track. For no apparent reason a wagon would suddenly become derailed whilst the train was proceeding normally, and the derailed vehicle would continue along, bouncing over the sleepers until it either fell to pieces or hit an area of points and crossings. In either case the train would break in two, and the rear portion would pile up into a heap of derailed and damaged wagons, spilling their contents far and wide. From BR's point of view, it was an expensive episode, and its customers were not very pleased at the loss, damage and delay which their freight suffered. From the Inspectorate's point of view there was always the danger that a passenger train on the next line would be too close to the accident to be stopped, and would plough into the wreckage. The beginning of the story might be taken to be the derailment and subsequent collision which occurred on the former Great Central main line between Rugby and Lutterworth on 11 February 1961. The 1.50am freight train from Woodford to Mottram was running at just over 50mph when the 26th vehicle, an empty pallet van, left the rails about a mile north of Rugby. The train ran on for another mile, with more vehicles becoming derailed, until the train broke in two. A few minutes later the 10.23pm passenger train York to Swindon ran into the wreckage and its engine overturned, killing the driver. Col Reed investigated the accident but could not find sufficient evidence to establish clearly the cause of the initial derailment. There had already been a number of pallet van derailments, and research was being carried out into the springing and suspension of the vans, which resulted in minor modifications being made. Col Reed commented that BR was examining the use of flares to give added warning of danger, and recommended that they should be adopted as soon as possible. The use of flares had been considered by the railways on many occasions in the previous half-century, but they had always decided to take no action on the matter, a stance from which they did not depart on this occasion, and from which they have never departed.

A similar accident occurred on 1 April 1963 just after 4.0pm, about two miles south of Weedon on the West Coast main line. The 2.18pm fitted freight train Camden to Glasgow Sighthill, diesel-hauled by Sulzer Type 2 No D5146, was running at slightly more than 55mph (the maximum speed allowed for that class of train) when the fifth vehicle, a lightly-loaded four-wheeled insulated fruit van with a 10ft wheelbase, left the rails. The driver was unaware of this, and the train ran on at speed under clear signals with the fruit van bouncing along, upright and in line, until its derailed wheels struck the points and crossings at Weedon, when it started to overturn on to the Up Main line just as the 'Royal Scot' express was approaching. Fortunately the express had been checked at the outer home signal and it was running towards the inner home signal at about 20mph when the collision occurred. No one was hurt and the express was not derailed.

The fruit van had a maximum speed of 60mph and should have been safe in the 2.18pm Camden to Sighthill but its springs were badly out of adjustment and only minor but rhythmic irregularities in the track were needed to increase oscillation to such an extent that derailment would ensue, despite those track irregularities being well within permitted tolerances. Col Robertson commented that the number of derailments such as this one had been causing concern for some time and BR accordingly had imposed a speed limit of 50mph from 16 April 1963 on all trains conveying short wheelbase vehicles.

As proof that the problem was not exclusively one of diesel haulage, there was a derailment the following year on 7 April 1964 in which the motive power involved was one of BR's splendid Class 9F 2-10-0s, No 92161. The train concerned was the 8.45pm fully fitted freight from Manchester Ancoats to Carlisle and it was coasting along the easy falling gradients from Appleby to Carlisle when the 17th vehicle, a 12-ton empty shock absorbing van, became derailed on plain track at a speed of between 55 and 60mph near Howe & Co's Sidings signalbox. Shortly afterwards the derailed van hit the points and crossings and pulled the whole of the second portion of 16 vehicles and brakevan into wholesale derailment. On investigation it was found that the cause was a combination of circumstances that were becoming familiar:

● A minor wagon defect (a weak spring).
● Excess speed (the limit for the train was 50mph but the engine was not equipped with a speedometer and it was a very dark night).
● Minor track defects within laid-down tolerances.

Following the derailment of an empty banana van near Steventon, on the Western Region between Didcot and Swindon on 21 January 1966, BR took what Lt-Col McNaughton referred to as a highly restrictive step of reducing the maximum permitted speed of all trains conveying 10ft wheelbase wagons to 45mph, even though it was known that this would have a most serious effect on traffic movement. However, despite this action the number of freight train derailments continued to increase apace, from 259 in 1966 to a peak of 383 in 1969, after which the figure fell back rapidly to 230 in 1972 and 146 in 1976. The problem was never satisfactorily resolved. It was eased by improved wagon maintenance and other steps but it gradually ceased to be a major problem with the rapid rundown in the number of short wheelbase wagons in the 1970s.

The cause of the phenomenon is now clear, but the knowledge would not have helped to provide a solution. Short wheelbase wagons had run for many years at speeds well in excess of 60mph, and without derailment, but they were wooden wagons running on conventional track, with bullhead rails on wooden sleepers. Both wagon and track were therefore flexible and could easily absorb any bumps or imperfections without causing oscillation or 'hunting' to be set up. Newer wagons had steel frames, and CWR track on concrete sleepers is far more rigid. This lack of flexibility in track and wagon, combined with the sustained high speeds achieved by diesel locomotives, and the higher speeds of freight trains in general due to the increased availability of brake-fitted wagons, were the roots of the problem to which it is clear there was no answer other than a new wagon suspension system, such as was installed on the emerging fleet of modern long wheelbase airbraked vehicles. One can only marvel at the streams of express freight trains, fish and meat trains which used to run up and down the East Coast main line at almost express passenger train speeds in times gone by, with never a thought of derailment. They were all 10ft wheelbase wagons.

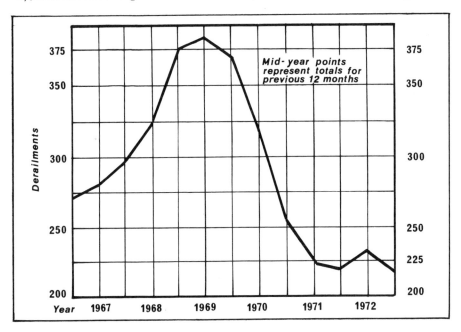

The other major area of worry in the 1960s concerned broken rails. After the number of cases had hovered around the 200-250 mark annually throughout the late 1950s-early 1960s, there was a sudden and dramatic increase from 1965 onwards to such an extent that the annual rate had doubled by 1969. The incidence of broken rails continued to increase throughout the 1970s.

Broken rails only occasionally led to a derailment but the most serious accident on BR in the last 30 years was caused by a broken rail at Hither Green on the Southern Region on 5 November 1967, when the 12-coach 19.43 diesel-electric multiple-unit train Hastings to Charing Cross was derailed at 70mph, killing 49 passengers. The 1968 total of 436 broken rails in plain line was made up as follows:

● Breaks at rail ends   200
● Breaks away from rail ends   109
● Breaks at welded joints   127

There were also 205 breaks in points and crossings.

It might be thought from reading this chapter that rail safety in the late 1960s had taken a serious downturn, and certainly many of the trends were adverse. It was a very worrying period, because although the number of serious accidents caused by errors of drivers and signalmen was on the decline, the new technical problems of freight train derailments and broken rails were not only getting worse year by year but there seemed to be no readily available solution.

Cols McMullen and Reed, who retired in 1968, must have been very disappointed at the situation they left behind. Col Robertson became the new CIO and he was joined by two new Inspecting Officers, Lt-Col A. G. Townsend-Rose and Maj C. F. Rose, who was the last Chief Inspecting Officer to have been an officer of the Royal Engineers. We shall see in the next chapter how they tackled the formidable and somewhat novel problems which faced them and BR.

Major C. F. Rose CBE
Chief Inspecting Officer: 1982-88

Born in 1926, Charles (Freddie) Rose started his railway career in 1942 as a trainee civil engineer with the Southern Railway Company. He was commissioned in the Royal Engineers in 1947 and for the next four years was engaged in railway construction, maintenance and operation in Palestine, Egypt and Libya. Thereafter he divided his time between railway work, including a year's secondment to British Railways in the late 1950s, and more general soldiering and military engineering work. His service took him to Germany, Korea, Kuwait and Thailand, where he was the engineer for a major road construction project close to the Laos border at the height of the Vietnam war.

He was selected for promotion to Lieutenant-Colonel in 1968 but elected to leave the Army and join the Railway Inspectorate as an Inspecting Officer. He was appointed Chief Inspecting Officer in 1982 and from 1986 combined this with chairmanship of the Channel Tunnel Safety Authority. He retired from the Inspectorate in 1988 but remained in the Department of Transport for a further year to continue his work with the Safety Authority. He is still involved with the Tunnel project, as a consultant.

Statistical Summary 1948-1968

Year	Miles of line open (BR & LTE)	No of train accidents	No of significant train accidents	No of passenger train Collisions	Derailments	No of passengers killed in train accidents
1948	19,853	1,293	—	65	47	39
1949	19,849	1,176	—	81	66	—
1950	19,797	1,156	—	60	56	11
1951	19,694	1,280	—	87	59	43
1952	19,580	1,243	—	83	43	111
1953	19,499	1,123	—	77	51	22
1954	19,445	1,197	—	73	53	—
1955	19,378	1,156	—	70	45	40
1956	19,288	1,226	—	80	40	—
1957	19,252	1,205	—	65	38	92
1958	19,192	1,186	—	63	49	18
1959	18,791	1,154	—	67	39	—
1960	18,597	1,175	415	59	33	6
1961	18,430	1,230	423	63	53	9
1962	17,687	1,348	391	52	37	20
1963	17,198	1,300	380	33	44	1
1964	16,206	1,209	348	28	28	5
1965	15,135	1,268	379	17	25	2
1966	13,935	1,358	402	22	30	—
1967	13,386	1,343	408	22	27	71
1968	n/a	1,405	461	15	31	10

Note:

In 1959 one passenger was killed whilst standing at an open window when struck by an open door on a passing train.

Statistical Summary 1948-1968 — *Continued*

Year	No of railway staff (BR & LTE) (000)	Train accidents	No of railway staff killed Movements	Total train miles (BR) (million)
1948	703	14	177	366
1949	648	6	182	381
1950	628	8	179	384
1951	622	4	154	376
1952	625	9	171	376
1953	616	7	178	379
1954	600	1	138	378
1955	586	8	154	363
1956	593	3	144	376
1957	596	4	147	382
1958	573	5	117	376
1959	541	8	136	371
1960	535	6	123	375
1961	523	10	134	373
1962	498	2	103	359
1963	462	12	87	348
1964	422	9	80	336
1965	388	5	84	311
1966	362	3	53	297
1967	341	5	60	285
1968	319	8	43	279

The New Railway

The year 1969 can confidently be said to be the start of the new railway era. The steam engine had been phased out the previous year. Modernisation of signalling was proceeding apace — Trent, Derby and Saltley power signalboxes were opened in 1969, and the Transport Act of 1968 had brought local authorities very substantially into the whole field of suburban passenger transport planning and financing. From now on the railways were not only technically more complex, but also politically so.

Keeping abreast of these major changes, and their effect upon safety, was the Railway Inspectorate, which in 1969 consisted of the Chief Inspecting Officer, Col J. R. H. Robertson (who retired in 1973), Lt-Col I. K. A. McNaughton (who succeeded Col Robertson and retired in 1982), Lt-Col A. G. Townsend-Rose (retired in 1986), and Maj C. F. Rose, who became Chief Inspecting Officer in 1982 and retired in 1988. Finally, the longest serving Inspecting Officer since Lt-Col Sir Alan Mount, who retired in 1949, was Maj P. M. Olver, who joined the Inspectorate in 1965 and retired only in 1989. Col Robertson was replaced in 1973 by Maj A. G. B. King, and the Inspectorate was strengthened in 1977 to cater for the increasing workload, by Maj C. B. Holden. The two latter officers are still active, and to Maj Holden belongs the distinction of being the last officer of the Corps of Royal Engineers to become a Railway Inspecting Officer.

The problems that faced the Inspectorate in its never-ending quest to improve safety standards on the railways were very much a mixture of old and new. The spread of AWS and power signalling with multiple-aspect colour-light signals and continuous track circuiting has certainly reduced the number of serious collisions caused either by signalmen's errors or by drivers passing signals at danger, indeed, of the 29 fatal train accidents on BR in the 21-year period 1969-1989 signalmen were involved in only three, a remarkable change from the situation of earlier days. However, drivers were still responsible wholly or partly in 15 cases and it has become very clear that not enough attention has been paid to, and not enough money invested in, measures to assist the driver.

It may perhaps be helpful to compare the decade 1980-89 with earlier decades, to see to what extent the causes of accidents have changed. In comparing the number of fatalities, and the number of fatal accidents, regard must be paid to the very great improvement in safety which has been achieved in the design and construction of modern coaches. In earlier years many passengers were killed in accidents who today might, and probably would, have survived, when coaches simply disintegrated, or where coach bodies became detached from their underframes; or, most terrible of all, when one coach was telescoped into the next destroying compartments and killing their occupants.

	1900-09	1930-39	1980-89
1 Number of fatal train accidents	31	23	12
2 Number of passengers killed	169	117	75
3 Number of cases in which the driver was wholly or partly responsible	17	14	5
4 Number of cases in which the signalman was wholly or partly responsible	10	11	2
5 Number of cases of a technical nature:			
Track and structures	2	2	3
Train (mechanical)	5	1	—
Signalling	1	—	1
6 Number of cases caused by obstructions, including accidents at level crossings	1	3	2
7 Number of passenger journeys in mid-point year (1905, 1935, 1985) (million)	1,199 excluding season tickets	1,249 excluding season tickets	1,385 including season tickets
8 Train mileage in mid-point year (million)	401	435	294

Notes:
 (i) In interpreting these figures, lines 1 to 6 refer only to those railways which are now part of British Rail, but lines 7 and 8 refer to all railways in Britain, including London Underground, Tyne & Wear Metro, etc.
 (ii) The 1900-9 figures in lines 7 and 8 include the whole of Ireland.
 (iii) In 1935, the number of season ticket journeys was estimated to be 448 million, giving a grand total for the year of 1,697 million passenger journeys.
 (iv) In 1985 British Rail passenger journeys, including season tickets, totalled 688 million. BR train miles were: passenger 203 million; freight 57 million.

It might be misleading to attempt to draw firm conclusions from a small number of accidents — but nevertheless, if the 1980-89 traffic levels are equated to those of 1930-39 there would appear to have been very little improvement over that 50-year period, either in the number of fatal train accidents or in the number of passengers killed. This is despite the very considerable investment in equipment to safeguard against errors made by drivers and signalmen, the effect of which is clearly demonstrated by the figures. The fact is that whilst the old, classical perils have been largely overcome, new perils have arisen consequent upon the introduction of new technology; also trains run faster, on lines of higher density.

1969, the start of our chapter, was a particularly bad year for derailments caused by buckles in continuously-welded rails. During June and July of that year there were no fewer than four, although fortunately they were all without fatality. The derailments took place as follows:

10 June Lichfield LMR	Electrically-hauled carflats
13 June Somerton WR	Paignton to Paddington express
15 June Lamington SCR	Freightliner
23 July Sandy ER	Down Tees-Tyne Pullman

This problem was the subject of a very lengthy and thorough investigation by Maj Rose, resulting in both an interim and a final report (the latter not appearing until 1974), which dealt admirably in detail with this technically complex matter. Both reports well repay study. BR took prompt action to deal with the problem, and whilst buckles still occur today they have been considerably reduced in number, although not completely eradicated, as the derailment of the 16.10 Glasgow to Euston express at Motherwell on 15 June 1986 demonstrated.

Broken rails, however, have proved a much more intractable problem, as the following figures show:

	1969	*1978*	*1988*
Number of breaks at rail ends	225	185	135
Number of broken welds	177	368	242
Number of breaks away from rail ends	105	210	177

Broken rails were responsible for two fatal train accidents in the 1980s, at Ulleskelf (ER) in 1981 and at Elgin (ScR) in 1983. A broken weld caused the derailment of the 20.25 Euston to Manchester express at Bushey on 16 February 1980; the train was travelling at almost 100mph, and the accident resulted in 19 passengers being seriously injured. However, the number of broken welds shown in the table above has to be set against a considerable increase in the number of such welds, and the rate of breaks per 1,000 miles has been halved since the early 1970s.

One of the most remarkable features of railway operating history has been the apparent reluctance of railway managements to take any action to help the driver in the three main fundamentals of his job:

● To obey the timetable.
● To keep within the speed limit of track and train.
● To stop when the signals tell him to do so.

131

Perhaps it sounds too easy, put like that, and generations of railway managers have possibly failed to have a complete conception of the demands placed upon drivers. If proof were required of that statement, then consider how little the railways have done to help drivers to run their trains more safely until circumstances have compelled them to do so. With the honourable exception of the Great Western, none of the railways was prepared to adopt ATC, and it was not until 1948, in the euphoria of the early days of nationalisation, that the decision was taken to equip the main lines with ATC (later known as AWS). Even then, progress was hardly dramatic. It was to be 10 years before installation commenced, and another 30 before the programme was complete, by which time about two-thirds of BR's track mileage had been dealt with. Long before then the weakness of the BR Automatic Warning System in failing to differentiate between single and double-yellow signals had become apparent. The GWR had already devised a means of achieving this with its ATC, but BR not only failed to incorporate the facility in its own system, despite considerable pressure from the Southern Region to do so, but, worse still, failed to modify its system when this flaw became apparent.

Yet again, the railway authorities failed to act until forced to do so by the weight of public pressure following the Purley accident on 4 March 1989, when the 12.17 EMU from Littlehampton to London Victoria ran past a danger signal at high speed and collided with the 12.50 EMU from Horsham to Victoria, killing five passengers and seriously injuring 32. There had been a similar accident at Wembley in 1984, when an evening commuter train collided with a freightliner train, killing three passengers, and there had been several other non-fatal collisions, but the implications were not acted upon.

The problem with the BR AWS system lies not just in its failure to differentiate between single and double yellow signals but also in the absence of any check that the driver has actually responded to the warnings that he has received. This of course is the ultimate safeguard, and it is incorporated in all modern systems. It would have prevented not only the accidents mentioned, but also others in which drivers for one reason or another failed to respond to the AWS warning. For example, there was an accident at Shields Junction near Glasgow Central in 1973 when the 21.35 EMU from Wemyss Bay ran into the back of the 21.10 DMU from Ayr, the driver having failed to react to caution and danger signals. It transpired that the driver was suffering from severe arterial disease and may have been taken ill suddenly when approaching Shields Junction, to such an extent that whilst he was sufficiently conscious to cancel the AWS warnings he could neither apply the brake nor release the Driver's Safety Device (DSD) which itself would have applied the brake. We can never be certain precisely what happened, because the driver was himself killed in the crash. The important fact is that the automatic warning system was ineffective, for the simple reason that it was not designed to cater for such a situation. BR has always maintained that its AWS is only an advisory system, which is perfectly correct, but it leaves too many loopholes for fate to exploit.

In his report into the 1984 Wembley collision, Maj Rose said that the fact that AWS had been unable to prevent the accident had important implications for safety, and that it had been apparent for some time that whilst AWS had proved a most important aid to drivers and had undoubtedly helped to reduce the number of collisions, it did not guard against incorrect cancellation of the kind that can arise when drivers are running under a sequence of cautionary signals — still less the 'unconscious' cancellation of the kind that apparently happened at Wembley. He also mentioned that the Inspectorate was already discussing with the British Railways Board, before the Wembley accident, the question of AWS and other aids to drivers and that these discussions were continuing. Maj Rose also drew attention quite forcibly to this question in his 1986 Annual Report, when he said:

'Whilst the overall state of railway safety during 1986 was not unsatisfactory I have to draw attention once again to the rising trend in the proportion of accidents caused by staff error. More than half of the serious or potentially serious collisions and derailments that did occur during 1986 were attributed to this cause and the number of signals passed at danger (including those where no accident resulted) continues to rise. British Rail are well aware of this and are currently analysing the figures in detail, with the help of outside consultants, to try to establish the underlying reasons. These studies should help the Board to decide on its future policy in respect of train control and operation. Should it follow the trend already established on many other European railways and go for some form of automatic train protection, or is the cost of such measures not worth the benefits they would bring? The question is a difficult one, and not only on grounds of cost, since much of BR is now equipped with a standard form of multiple-aspect signalling and associated advance warning system, much of it with years of service left before it needs renewal . . . Nevertheless I believe the time has come when the Board must face the questions and seek answers that will enable it to establish a clear policy for the future. I have made clear in previous reports the Inspectorate's view that more needs to be done to assist the driver in the cab.'

The Wembley report is dated 21 February 1986 and it was not to be long before another AWS loophole was expensively demonstrated. On Friday 19 September 1986 the 17.00 express from Euston to Manchester, hauled by electric locomotive No 86429, ran past a danger signal at Colwich and came to a stand with the locomotive partly across the junction to Stoke and directly in the path of the 17.20 express from Liverpool to Euston, also electrically-hauled by locomotive No 86211, which was hard on the scene approaching at almost 100mph. The unfortunate driver of the Liverpool train had no time to do anything and lost his life in the ensuing crash, which flung the carriages of his train in a jumbled heap. Looking at photographs of the crash one would have expected a lengthy death-roll, especially as there were almost 900 passengers in the two trains, but there were no fatalities at all among the passengers, and there can be no more eloquent testimony to the life-preserving qualities of modern coaching stock than that. However, it was inevitable that there would be many injuries, and 32 passengers were detained in hospital.

It appears that the driver of the Manchester train had been confused by a new junction signalling system of flashing yellow lights which had only recently been installed, and assumed that the road was set for him to proceed on to the Stoke line, but he was mistaken, and the signals only allowed him to proceed as far as, but not on to, the junction. Here again, the precise details of the cause are of no real consequence. What matters is that AWS did not prevent the accident, because it was not designed to do so. After the Colwich accident it was very clear that the existing AWS was no longer adequate and that a system was needed that would ensure that a train stopped at a danger signal irrespective of anything the driver did, or did not do, but it was not until the Purley accident that BR decided to take action.

The driver's duty to keep within the speed limits of track and train has already been mentioned, and the history of railways is marked with instances where drivers have failed to do so. It is not at all surprising that this is the case, because until BR days few locomotives were provided with speedometers, and until recently drivers received little or no advance warning that they were approaching sharp curves. The change came about following a derailment at Morpeth on 7 May 1969, when the 19.40 sleeper from King's Cross to Edinburgh attempted to go round the 40mph curve at 80mph. Five passengers and a travelling ticket inspector were killed, and there were many injuries.

Col Robertson held the public inquiry into the Morpeth derailment and took the view that on a high speed line the driver of an express train should receive a special warning that he was approaching a severe speed restriction on the open line, which he suggested ought to be provided where a reduction of speed of one-third or more was required on lines where speeds of 75mph and above were permitted. He further suggested that this warning should take the form of an illuminated advance warning board, which should be installed at braking distance from the speed restriction, and that a permanent AWS-type magnet should be placed between the rails 200yd before the warning board, to draw the driver's attention to it.

BR adopted these proposals but they did not go far enough. A speed of 75mph was too high for the dividing line between the provision and non-provision of warning equipment. Several derailments had occurred on lower speed lines, and lines with a maximum speed of 60mph were subsequently embraced in the arrangement. However, there was a special situation in the Up (southbound) direction at Morpeth. The sharp curve was approached by a series of descending speed restrictions, firstly to 80mph, then to 70mph, and therefore it did not fall within the parameters laid down. Consequently, no warning equipment was provided in the Up direction, leaving a safety loophole which was cruelly exploited on the night of 23-24 June 1984. The driver of the 19.50 sleeping car express from Aberdeen to King's Cross, the 'Night Aberdonian', failed to reduce speed and passed through Morpeth station at between 85 and 90mph. The train hit the 50mph curve and shot off at a tangent, straight towards some bungalows, which were damaged. Astonishingly, not a single passenger was killed. Action was subsequently taken to deal with such situations involving a 'cascade' of speed restrictions.

Drivers are expected to be aware of all permanent speed limits, but when temporary restrictions of speed have to be imposed, usually on track awaiting or undergoing repair, the driver is informed beforehand in a weekly booklet containing all the temporary speed restrictions on the lines he has to work over. In addition, a warning sign is erected at the side of the line, sufficiently far back to enable the driver to brake in time, and the actual site of the speed restriction is marked by further lineside signs. These signs are illuminated at night, originally by paraffin oil, then later by bottled gas, and now by electric batteries.

On the night of 5-6 June 1975 the 23.30 sleeper from Euston to Glasgow approached Nuneaton at 80mph and became derailed on a 20mph temporary speed restriction. The lights at the warning board had gone out and the driver thought that the restriction must therefore have been removed. A classic case of 'the light that failed', beloved by 19th century dramatists.

The lights had gone out because all the gas had been used, but for some time the Inspectorate had been pressing BR for improvements in the method of illumination and general appearance of warning boards, and it is surprising that there had not been similar accidents previously. An examination was made of Continental practice and it was found that several railway administrations there made use of the automatic warning device employed in the signalling system in order to alert drivers to the fact that they were approaching a temporary speed restriction. After some hesitation, and worries about possible side-effects, BR decided to place a permanent magnet of the AWS type, between the rails 200yd before the warning board, a simple, elegant and effective solution, and one which drivers have welcomed, as it removes a great deal of anxiety from their daily lives.

After the collision at Hixon level crossing in 1968 the automation of Britain's 2,000 or so public level crossings came to an abrupt halt, although the reasons for automation had not been removed. Quite the reverse, in fact. But, following the report of the Hixon Inquiry, held by Mr E. B. Gibbens QC, the principles to be adopted in the installation of automatic level crossings were amplified, which had the effect of making them so expensive to install that it was no longer cost-effective for BR to do so. There followed 10 years of stalemate, during which the number of automatic half-barrier (AHB) installations increased only from 201 in 1968 to 234 in 1978. It was clear to everyone that something had to be done to find a solution, and accordingly in 1977 Lt-Col McNaughton, now the Chief Inspecting Officer, arranged with BR to set up a joint working party with the following aim:

'To consider ways in which methods of level crossing protection can be further developed in Great Britain, taking into account the cost and the need to maintain an adequate and publicly acceptable standard of safety — and to make recommendations.'

Lt-Col Townsend-Rose was appointed joint chairman with a BR representative, and the working party visited a number of Continental railways. Its report, issued in 1978, not only recommended some easement of the onerous conditions in regard to AHBs, thus allowing a further 100 gated crossings to be converted to AHB in the next few years, but also suggested that a new type of level crossing automation system should be introduced, similar to an AHB installation but without barriers, and with reliance being placed entirely upon the road user's obedience to the flashing red road traffic signals at the level crossing. These new crossings were called Automatic Open Crossings (AOCR) and there were 44 in use by 1986. However, that year the doubtful wisdom of relying upon road users infallibly to obey the traffic lights was demonstrated by a very serious accident at Lockington, on the Hull to Bridlington line, when a DMU became derailed after a small van came on to the level crossing in front of it. Eight passengers and an occupant of the van were killed.

There was often a strong, and to some extent illogical, local feeling against the automation of level crossings, and there was serious public disquiet following the Lockington disaster. The Secretary of State for Transport therefore felt impelled to have yet another independent inquiry into the safety of level crossings, and appointed Prof P. F. Stott 'to review the safety record of automatic open level crossings, to consider the lessons gained from the experience so far and to make recommendations . . .'

His report, dated 17 July 1987, generally recommended some tightening of the conditions applicable to automatic open crossings, which has had the result of requiring the conversion of some of the existing installations to AHBs. Experience has shown that the motorist cannot be relied upon to obey the traffic lights at level crossings without fail, and deliberate disregard is by no means unknown. The upshot of all this, however, is that there are still over 400 gated level crossings, and 600 with manually-controlled lifting barriers, but in the ultimate reckoning it is the safety of the rail passengers which has to be assured.

It will have been noted that both of the major accidents at public level crossings have been followed by a review carried out by neither BR nor the Railway Inspectorate, but by a private individual. This has been done in the name of independence, and undoubtedly with some justification, as both road and rail sections of the Department of Transport were deeply involved in drawing up the principles to be applied to the automation of level crossings, and it would not have been appropriate for the Department to have been seen as both judge and defendant. The 1871 Regulation of Railways Act makes provision for this more formal type of inquiry, either held by an Inspecting Officer assisted by a QC or similar person, or vice versa. The procedure was invoked several times in the 1870s but the practice was abandoned as it was found to be cumbersome, time-wasting, and less effective than the usual form of inquiry held by an Inspecting Officer without interference from the legal profession.

It is over 100 years since the formal public inquiry mechanism was last invoked in the case of a collision between trains, but the public pressure for a 'full independent inquiry' following a serious collision at Clapham Junction in December 1988 was so great that the Secretary of State for Transport concurred, and a formal inquiry was established under a QC, Anthony Hidden. Public opinion is not always a good guide, especially in complex matters such as railway safety, and people seem to be unaware of the fact that the Railway Inspectorate is completely separate from, and independent of, the British Railways Board, as well as enjoying total independence on safety matters within the Department of Transport, and in this respect it is able to give unfettered advice to Ministers. It would have been entirely appropriate for an Inspecting Officer to have held the inquiry into the Clapham accident. There was no precedent for the Secretary of State's decision, as every inquiry into a railway accident in the whole 150 years of the Inspectorate's existence (excepting the two special cases of the Tay Bridge collapse and the Hixon level crossing accident) has been held by an Inspecting Officer.

To some extent, the Inspectorate is in a period of change, after almost a century and a half of remarkable stability. When Maj Rose retired as Chief Inspecting Officer in 1988 he was replaced by Mr Robin Seymour, who had previously been employed by the Health & Safety Executive. This was an unprecedented step on two counts:

● No previous chief had been appointed, who had not already had considerable experience as an Inspecting Officer.
● Every previous chief had been an officer of the Corps of Royal Engineers.

Mr R. J. Seymour MA
Chief Inspecting Officer: 1988 to date

Robin Seymour joined the Railway Inspectorate as Chief Inspecting Officer in 1988, having previously been with the Health & Safety Executive. He had been working since 1984 as Her Majesty's Deputy Chief Inspector of Factories in the Hazardous Substances Division.

A Cambridge graduate, Mr Seymour served as HM Inspector of Factories in Yorkshire, Lancashire and the West Midlands dealing with health and safety in a wide range of industries, before being appointed District Inspector for Stirling in 1966.

In 1973 he moved to the London headquarters of the Inspectorate, and on the establishment of the Health & Safety Executive he worked for several years in the Executive's Safety Policy Division, later serving as Area Director of the Inspectorate's North West London area. In 1982 he returned to the Inspectorate HQ on promotion to Deputy Chief Inspector with responsibility for Area offices in Scotland and the North of England; he moved to the Railway Inspectorate six years later.

Mr A. Cooksey BSc (Hons), CEng, MICE

Alan Cooksey, 48, is a Chartered Civil Engineer and an Inspecting Officer of Railways. He joined the Railway Inspectorate in 1975 as an Employment Inspector, having previously been employed on the London Midland Region of British Rail as a civil engineer mainly concerned with bridge and electrification works. He was promoted to the new post of Deputy Chief Inspecting Officer in 1988.

For reasons already given, it was of course inevitable that the source of Inspecting Officers would change, and the process had indeed started in 1982 with the appointment as an Assistant Inspecting Officer of Mr Alan Cooksey, who had previously been a Principal Railway Employment Inspector, and it is likely that this will be the normal source of Inspecting Officers in the future, after they have had some experience as Railway Employment Inspectors. These Inspectors are concerned with the safety of staff employed on the railways and were established in 1900 following the passing of the Railway Employment (Prevention of Accidents) Act that year. There is not room within these pages to deal with the history and activities of the Employment Inspectors, indeed they deserve a book of their own, but they were originally established owing to the high death rate and the number of injuries among railway staff. In 1900, 24 railwaymen were killed in train accidents and 559 from other causes, a lamentable record. There has been since then a steady and continuous improvement, to such an extent that only two railwaymen were killed in train accidents in 1988, and 14 from all other causes, which seems very creditable, considering the nature and variety of the daily hazards to which many staff are exposed, even though the number of railway staff employed in 1987 was only a quarter of the number employed in 1900.

One other development which ought to be mentioned, because of its impact on the Inspectorate, is the Health & Safety at Work Act 1974, which was passed 'to make further provision for securing the health, safety and welfare of persons at work, for protecting others against risks to health or safety in connection with the activities of persons at work . . .'

Whilst the Act was not specifically intended to be applied to railway employment, it does so along with the generality of other employment, even though the provisions of the 1900 Railway Employment Act are still in force. To avoid duplication, the Department of Transport has concluded an Agency Agreement with the Health & Safety Commission in respect of the application of the Act to railway workers, and under this agreement the Railway Inspectorate carries out those functions relating to 'the health, safety and welfare of persons at work engaged in the operation, inspection or maintenance of any statutory railway, and protecting people other than those at work against risks to health or safety arising out of or in connection with these activities'.

Staff safety is dealt with by the Railway Employment Inspectors, but the sting in the tail of the 1974 Act lies in the phrase 'and protecting people other than those at work' which could be construed to mean passengers. The previous legislation, under which the Railway Inspectorate operates, has no enforcement provisions in this respect. The Inspectorate can only make recommendations, unlike the 1974 Act, which has a battery of penal sanctions. There are siren voices calling for the Railway Inspectorate to use these penal sanctions to enforce changes, rather than to use its customary process of recommendation and persuasion, but anyone contemplating this drastic and disastrous measure would do well to consider the consequences, which were clearly spelt out when consideration was being given in earlier days to providing the Inspectorate with greater powers.

A moment's thought will clearly show the serious pitfalls of encouraging the Inspectorate to use the powers of the Health & Safety at Work Act to insist on its recommendations being adopted. The result would ultimately be to make the Inspectorate responsible for safety standards, equipment and procedures on BR, relieving BR from that responsibility. There would then need to be established a separate and independent Accident Investigation Department, because it would clearly be inappropriate for an Inspector wielding as a matter of course the enforcement provisions of the Health and Safety legislation to investigate accidents which might well have resulted from its own decisions, or lack of action. Furthermore, for the enforcement procedures to be used in this way by the Inspectorate could commit BR to an expenditure of many millions of pounds, taking the Inspectorate into the field of general railway management. It is most regrettable that the 1974 Act has blurred the old and well-established procedures and traditions, and this process of reshaping is still going on, indeed it seems likely that further organisational changes are imminent and that the Railway Inspectorate will be transferred from the Department of Transport to the Health & Safety Executive. If this is merely a change of address, and if the Inspectorate continues to operate as it does today under existing railway legislation, no great harm may result, but if the mood of the Inspectorate were to change from one of safety audit and co-operation in the interests of the common goal of greater safety, to one of high-handed interference backed up by threats of prosecution; and if co-operation were replaced by remote coercion there is no guarantee that safety would be improved. What is certain is that the valuable relationship which has been built up between the Inspectorate and the British Railways Board would be seriously impaired.

As things stand at present BR is responsible for the safety of passengers. The 1962 Transport Act says so. No sensible person could possibly contemplate changing that and making a government department or quango responsible. After all, the success of the present system can be seen in BR's excellent safety record – only 12 fatal train accidents in the last 10 years and only 75 passengers killed. In the same period, over 50,000 people have been killed on the roads, with no great outcry. Politicians and the media would do well to remember that fact, the next time there is a serious railway accident, and leave the Inspectorate to get on with the job which it has performed with such distinction and professional skill for the last 150 years.

And what of the future? What are the safety problems still facing BR and the Railway Inspectorate? Safety levels, after many years of improvement, appear to have reached a plateau, as the following table shows.

Years	No of passenger train collisions (annual average)	No of passenger train derailments (annual average)
1950-59	72	47
1960-69	32	33
1970-79	14	25
1980-88	17	28

Note: The figures include all railways, not just BR.

Reductions in the railway network, the widespread introduction of the automatic warning system, the elimination of steam and the modernisation of signalling have all played a part in the improvement in the figures, but these were all largely achieved by 1980, and the question is 'What more can be done to improve the record still further?' Do the causes of the fatal accidents in the 1980s give us any clue? Let us briefly look at them:

1981	Ulleskelf	Broken weld in rail.
	Seer Green	Signalman's error. Excessive speed by driver after having been cautioned.
1983	Elgin	Broken rail at fishbolt hole.
	Wrawby	Signalman's error.
1984	Polmont	Animals straying on the line.
	Wembley Central	Driver passed a signal at danger. AWS ineffective.
	Eccles	Driver passed a signal at danger. No AWS.
1986	Lockington	Van driver failed to obey the flashing red lights at an automatic open level crossing.
1987	Glanrhyd	Bridge collapse.
1988	Clapham Junction	Error by signal engineering technician.
1989	Purley	Driver passed a signal at Danger, AWS ineffective.
	Glasgow Bellgrove	Driver passed a signal at danger. Guard failed to observe the signal before giving 'Train ready to start' bell ring to driver.

Of these 12 cases, four – Wembley, Eccles, Purley and Bellgrove – would have been avoided by the new Automatic Train Protection system which BR says it intends to introduce, although it is likely to be several years before it is in use on a sufficiently wide scale to have a real impact.

Of the others, it would be vain to expect to eradicate broken welds and rails, and equally vain to expect that bridges will never collapse, that large animals will never stray on to the line, that motorists will never ever go on to a level crossing at the same time as a train, and that none of the 100,000 or so railwaymen will ever be careless, or make a mistake or an error of judgement of a sort that could not realistically have been foreseen and guarded against.

Railway passengers owe a great debt to the Railway Inspectorate for its part in achieving the very high standards of safety which now exist in the daily operation of thousands of trains. The sheer professionalism of the Inspectorate, its constancy and ability to take a long and detached view, its proper sense of proportion and realism, and its refusal to get excited when disaster strikes have made it one of the finest examples of the government regulation of a great industry that has ever existed. Perhaps this 150th anniversary would be a suitable time to resurrect the practice which existed up to World War 2 of conferring a Knighthood on the Chief Inspecting Officer. It would give the Inspectorate that extra degree of status which is important and would show that the government recognised the importance of the Inspectorate and valued its work. Let us also hope that in another 150 years the railways will still be there and enjoying prosperity, and let us equally hope that they will still be watched over, so far as safety is concerned, by a small and dedicated body of men known as the Railway Inspectorate, still acting under the powers of simple and well-proven railway legislation. Governments please note.

Let us also, as a nation, be mature enough to accept, without complacency, that accidents will continue to occur, and adult enough to do so without the over-reaction which unfortunately occurs all too often today. Indeed, let us just be thankful that serious accidents are now so rare. And let us salute the Railway Inspectorate on its 150th anniversary for the valuable part it has played in that achievement.

Index of Accidents

Index of Accidents — *Continued*

Index of Accidents — *Continued*

Index of Acts of Parliament

General Index